FIFTY WORDS
OF
ENCOURAGEMENT
JUST FOR YOU

VOLUME I

FIFTY WORDS
—— OF ——
ENCOURAGEMENT
JUST FOR YOU

PASTOR KEN REED

ARPress
ILLUMINATING IDEAS
EMPOWERING VOICES

ARPress
45 Dan Road Suite 5
Canton MA 02021

Hotline: 1(888) 821-0229
Fax: 1(508) 545-7580

Ordering Information:

Quantity sales. Special discounts are available on quantity purchases by corporations, associations, and others. For details, contact the publisher at the address above.

Printed in the United States of America.

ISBN-13:   Softcover   979-8-89330-531-9
            eBook   979-8-89330-533-3
            Hardcover   979-8-89330-532-6

Library of Congress Control Number: 2024900564

RECOMMENDATIONS

The understanding of words is the foundation of all communication. Words create pictures, and in order to create a masterpiece, it is of vital importance that we use the right words at the right time with the right meaning and proper application.

When it comes to using and applying the right words to create a beautiful picture, you need a great wordsmith. You need someone God has given this gift to. Pastor Ken is that someone. His understanding, depth, and grasp of words are a blessing. By using this tool during your devotions, the Holy Spirit will paint for you a clear picture of the intended meaning resulting in clarity of thought. As a brother and friend, I highly recommend this devotional. It is another great tool to help us see and understand with clarity the intended meaning as we feed our spirit. Invest in this devotional as you seek to grow.

Rev. Dr. David A. Spencer Pastor, author,
coach, and public speaker

In a time when uncertainty, fear, and concern seem to rule each day, we search for answers, peace of mind, and a break from the trek through this wilderness that surrounds us.

For me, it's a few moments dwelling on what really matters. as I am able to put the world aside and spend these moments contemplating Pastor Ken Reed's *Fifty Words of Encouragement.*

In it, he speaks directly to our yearning hearts with beautifully flowing text, helping us to better understand how to manage our earthly walk as Christians in a secular world.

Pastor Ken demonstrates his skill and knowledge of human nature by aptly describing our wants and desires, and how they fare within the scope of Christian values. He does not shy away from the truth even when painful because he understands this truth is vital if we are to walk with our Lord.

In *Fifty Words of Encouragement Just for You*, Pastor Ken demonstrates his ability to explain scripture in a way that leaves us feeling edified, fulfilled, enriched, and at peace. He accomplishes this with the use of subtle metaphors woven together with easy-to-understand declamatory phrases, ones which often come to mind before I sleep at night.

Whether you are a believer or not, I would recommend spending a few moments each day in Pastor Ken Reed's *Fifty Words of Encouragement Just for You*. If you are not a believer, these moments can open a door to a new life of commitment, appreciation, gratitude, and peace. If you are a believer, each word can enrich your understanding of Christian values and how they impact the way we see ourselves within our secular society. In either case, you will be blessed as you eagerly anticipate the next word of encouragement.

Randolph F. Berkson Operations manager WVNE-WILD

760 and 1090 AM/101.5 FM,

Worcester, Springfield, Boston

CONTENTS

IMMATURITY

To delay or cease the normal growth cycle; a state of being incomplete or underdeveloped.

Observing young children as they interact with their siblings and/or peers provides a most unique point of understanding for you and me.

On many occasions, there can be abstract and obvious displays of immature behaviors expressing themselves through these young, innocent lives.

We've watched the disputes over ownership of broken pencils, headless and armless dolls, and toy cars with no wheels.

We've observed the many mood swings of little ones appearing to suffer complete devastation because someone other than themselves consumed that last snack.

We can only imagine how much more our heavenly Father observes in you and me through His unobstructed view of seeing, knowing, and discerning all things.

There is no creature hidden from his sight, but all things are naked and open to the eyes of Him to whom we must give an account [some translations read, "With whom we have an account"]. (Hebrews 4:13)

Are we maturing? Are our lives presently on God's track, or are we refusing, for whatever reason, to move ahead into God's call and construct for our growth?

1 Corinthians 3:6–9 states that "it is man's ability to plant and water, but only God has the capacity to make things grow."

I don't believe we've actually ever seen growth because growth only functions within God's dimension; it is supernatural. What we have observed <u>is the result of growth and not growth itself</u>.

Our loving, heavenly Father has tailor-made a specific environment for your growth. And because He is perfect, the environment in which He has established for you is perfectly suited for your development and maturity.

Beloved, are you surrendering to God's design for you, or are you still contending for your own image, quietly pushing for your personal preferences and self-exaltation?

<u>Carefully consider the following scriptures and final thoughts:</u>

Hebrews 5:11 says, "God has much to say about this, but we are incapable of hearing because of immaturity." Verse 12 says we should now be ready to instruct but instead are still in need of being instructed. Verse 13 says we have been living on milk and not solid food.

Verse 14 declares that solid food is for the mature and that maturity develops through constant use.

Hebrews 6:1 encourages us to "leave the elementary teachings about Christ, and go on to maturity," ultimately fulfilling <u>our unique role in the body of Christ</u> of being lights shining in dark places and people who demonstrate God's kingdom.

Beloved, we must continually trust the faithfulness of God. It is He who chose to begin His work in you and me, and it is He who will continue His work unto its completion.

Let's be cognizant that our motivations are not that quiet push for personal gratification but, like Jesus, from the heart declare, *Father, not my will but your will be done*.

As always, in His love, Pastor Ken Reed

FRAME

A ridged structure that surrounds or encloses a supporting border, providing form and shape.

When building any structure, whether on a grand or modest scale, the process and procedures are generally as follows:

1. A full and official rendering (i.e., an architectural drawing of the finished product is undertaken). This drawing can be understood as the vision or purpose.

2. The location is secured and prepared (the clearing of land, etc.).

3. The foundation, a more substantial building, requires *a significantly deeper foundation*. After the foundation is established, the structure can begin to be framed.

Every other phase of construction is governed by the boundaries of the frame. The frame determines every internal and external design of the structure. The frame is the physical presence of the vision.

Even those who are to inhabit the structure upon completion live within the boundaries of the frame.

By faith, we understand that the visible and invisible worlds were framed by the Word of God. So that the things which are seen [i.e., the physical dimension] were not made with things which are visible or physical. (Hebrews 11:3 NKJV)

Prayerfully consider these next scriptures and comments:

And the Word became flesh and dwelt among us, so much so, that we beheld His Glory, the Glory as of the only begotten of the Father, full of Grace and truth. (John 1:14)

As new creations in Christ Jesus, we must know and believe God's Word is always in the process of becoming itself inside us.

He who began the work continues it to completion. (Philippians 1:6)

In John 1:14, the "eternal Word" was framed within the womb of a young virgin.

And Mary said to the angel of the Lord, "Be it unto me according to your word." (Luke 1:38)

So, after God's natural process and perfect timing (nine months), the framing was complete.

His invisible spoken Word became a physical manifestation, namely Jesus, the Anointed One.

Everything within God's kingdom is framed by His spoken Word and, at His appointed time, *becomes the physical expression of His perfect will.*

By the word of the Lord, were the heavens made, their starry host by the breath of His mouth. (Psalm 33:6)

Who can speak and have it happen, if the Lord has not commanded it. Is it not from the mouth of the Lord, that both good things and calamities proceed? (Lamentations 3:37–38)

Beloved, we are designed to live in two dimensions, first the spiritual then the physical. Within the physical realm, time exists, so everything has a specific point of occurrence (past, present, or future), hence our need for "faith and patience when inheriting God's promises" (Hebrews 6:12).

But in God's spiritual kingdom, time is nonexistent, so every- thing is always now. <u>We always start at the finish line</u>.

> *And God said...and it was so.* (Genesis 1:29–30)

Beloved, let us diligently and intentionally practice trusting the Lord and not our own sense of timing and reasoning.

<u>Remember this warning</u>!

For indeed the Gospel was preached to us, as well as to them, but the word preached did not profit them...because they who heard it, *did not mix faith with it.* (Hebrews 4:2; emphasis added)

> *As always, in His love,* Pastor Ken Reed

RELATIONSHIP

A state of being connected by blood, marriage, or acquaintance.

The Lord God said it is not good that man should be alone I will make him a helper *comparable* to him. (Genesis 2:18; emphasis added)

Entering into a relationship with someone is almost always intriguing and potentially exciting. Unfortunately, because of our fallen nature, the initial triggers of attraction are usually stimulated by a focus on ourselves (i.e., *our own brokenness*).

Developing any relationship is more complex than many of us can ever imagine. On most occasions, the excitement of our experience is simply a response to the prospect *that we have now discovered someone or something who can satisfy our longings.*

As you continue to engage each other, you, in fact, begin the assessment of their qualities; you can see and imagine the possibility of these qualities being used to serve you.

Beloved, I know that this might appear to be harsh, but it is not my intention to be such. Nor do I believe it is your intention that self-centeredness should frame your relationships. *We can still be vulnerable to the influences of corruption even when we don't intend to be.* In almost every scenario we engage in, good or bad, our focus tends to be through the lens of: *"How can it serve and make me better?"*

Beloved, whether we realize it or not, many of us view even God in such a manner. We have attempted to develop a relationship with Him using this same construct.

In today's culture, most relationships have an intensely short shelf life ranging from six months to about three years. And any time after this period, that is, once one's initial needs and longings have been satisfied, the relationship can begin to take a turn for the worse. And the same cycle starts all over again. "This present relation- ship is no longer adding anything *to me* and *is now become nothing but frustration and disappointment.*

A God-established relationship is never about what you add to me. Its focus is always on how I care for you.

I must continually look to God for the fulfillment of my internal longings. The Father knows just how to shape your partner so that the two become one flesh.

A one-flesh relationship is foreign to most of us simply because of its supernatural construct. There is a disconnect in our understanding as to *why the man did not disassociate himself from the woman in the garden.*

We imagine the kinds of actions or decisions Adam should've or could've taken to change everything.

Now, because the first Adam was one with his bride, he was not able to separate himself from her. This is expressed in our relationship with Jesus, the second Adam. We are now His bride, and whenever we sin, *He does not separate Himself from us.*

Where sin abounded God's grace abounded even more.
(Romans 5:20)

The second Adam also declares, "I will never leave you nor forsake you even until the end of the age" (Hebrews 13:5). You cannot protect yourself from the risk of pain or betrayal in any human relationship.

The secret to real love is always about allowing yourself to become vulnerable, trusting God's timing and choice for you.

It was God who tailor-made the woman for the man, and it was God who brought her to him. God loves you and has already prepared everything you'll need in this life, <u>even your relationships</u>.

As always, in His love, Pastor Ken Reed

COMPLAIN

To express dissatisfaction or annoyance about something (a real or imagined state of suffering); to find fault, protest, or grumble.

In this present-day culture, with the abundance of highly educated advanced thinkers, access to worldwide information, and the construct of constitutionally authorized free speech, and the articulation of our personal preferences has taken a place of "God-like pro- portions" in the average individual's life. (By the way, I am aware that in writing the article, I'm engaged in this very function.) However, every event, situation, or happening seems to demand our evaluation as if a failure to be verbally involved would mean our immediate demise or result in the complete loss of personal worth and identity. Now it is to the believer (i.e., one who has been born again, who is a new creation [a new species of being] in Christ Jesus) that these next comments are directed. James 1:19 says, *"We [the believer] should be quick to listen and slow to speak and slow to anger."*

According to Scripture, <u>we are no longer of this world</u>; we are called to be lights that shine in dark places.

Many a time, our struggle comes because of our self-protective focus on ourselves and the things appearing to provide immediate comfort, especially a way of escape from any sufferings, injustice, etc. It's impossible to trust the Lord when your focus is on yourself.

Consider this… God delivered Israel from the claws of the Egyptian empire and brought them through perilous places in the wilderness.

Opening the Red Sea and bringing extraordinary deliverance on their behalf, He had clearly demonstrated Himself as being *"the only wise and true God"* (Romans 16:27). In a similar fashion, He has shown himself to each of us.

However, only three days after deliverance from their enemy, at the rivers of Marah (t*he place of bitterness, complaint, and grumbling*), their desire/thirst for comfort was delayed, and immediately resentment and anger were expressed in the form of complaining and grumbling.

They thought it to be Moses's failure in leadership in bringing them to fresh water, but God says it was His choice in the place and method to provide for them. (By the way, God's choices are always perfect.)

The people's hearts became bitter just like the water; they had forgotten it was God who was directing their paths and that it was He who scheduled them to be in this dry and difficult place.

Beloved, please be warned and be careful not to speak foolishly out of a bitter heart regarding your present situation.

For it is God who has begun a work in you,
and it is God who continues that work until
the completion of His purpose.

(Philippians 1:6)

Remember, beloved, *we do not belong to ourselves but have been bought with the price, so our lives are not our own* (1 Corinthians 6:20). Let's not be as infants who whine or cry at the slightest discomfort but a people whose focus is on the faithfulness of God Almighty and a people who rejoice in the Lord not for everything but in every- thing, knowing that He is our faithful deliver and that "no weapon that sets itself against us will be successful" (Isaiah 54:17).

As always, in His love, Pastor Ken Reed

ANXIETY

A negative feeling usually accommodated by tension, nervousness, and uncertainty about the outcome of an imminent event or the near future.

Within this fast-paced, corrupt, and seductive culture is where our heavenly Father has set His church (i.e., you and me). Acts 17:26 says, *"God determined the time set for us, and the exact places where we should live."*

We are called to live in this world, without being of this world (i.e., lights shining in dark places).

However, on a variety of occasions, we can find ourselves being frustrated and influenced by various levels of anxiety. We all tend to express <u>this distraction</u> in a range of ways: some with handwringing and heart palpitations, some with annoyance and impatience, some through evicting others and isolating themselves, and some through internal scrutinizing of every personal failure in their life (i.e., self-pity and depression).

Anxiety is subtle in its deployment; it is cleverly hidden just below the surface and is woven into the fibers of our daily lives.

It easily functions within the constructs of our professions (especially ministry-related ones), our home life, parenting children, our marital relationships, and even our personal development.

By becoming a distraction, anxiety accomplishes its primary goal. It causes a shift in our focus from trusting the faithfulness, wisdom, and timing of God to the futility of self-reliance and self-management.

During this time of distraction, we are unwittingly wrestling with God for the responsibility of providing protection for us.

In this context, consider now Philippians 4:6–7 (emphasis added): "Do not be anxious about anything but in every situation by prayer with thanksgiving, present your requests to God. And the peace of God, which transcends all understanding, will guard your hearts and your minds in Christ Jesus."

When we are being distracted by anxiety, God's supernatural peace, though available to us, is now technically unavailable because we began to react emotionally and physically to the pressures we are facing. Consider this final example.

The Israelites, at the mouth of the Red Sea, had a similar experience of pressure and anxiety. On hearing and seeing the vast army approaching, they scrambled to manage their own escape, and upon realizing there was no way out, they succumbed to anxiety's full control. They even became threatening to Moses. (By the way, it was God, not man, who led them to where they were.)

God's Word to them is the same Word to you and me today.

Exodus 14:13 declares, "Do not fear, stand still, and see the deliverance of the Lord, the enemy that you see today [i.e., that which is causing your anxiety], you will not see again [that was the last time they ever saw Pharaoh]." Verse 14 continues, "The Lord will fight for you; you need only to be still."

Satan's most successful strategy against you and me today is distraction. With a ceaseless barrage of exposure to chaos, confusion, and contradictions, our singular focus on Christ is continuously being pressured. Distractions do cause a subtle shift in our focus from the one who is faithful above all to someone else (i.e., ourselves). "Standing still" is a reminder of our helplessness to protect ourselves. Philippians 4:7 says, "It is God's peace, that is responsible for guarding our hearts and our minds."

Beloved, He loves you. He is trustworthy and most faithful, so remember, "no weapon formed against you can prosper" (Isaiah 54:17). Be at peace in His faithfulness and love for you.

As always, in His love, Pastor Ken Reed

CHOSEN

To select from a collection; to single out of a group; to be specific or to elect; to pick; to prefer.

As new creations in Christ Jesus, you and I are specifically chosen. This inconceivable privilege and honor are not bestowed upon just anyone. *Although all are invited, only the chosen may attend.* There is, however, no valid justification for our being selected because we, like all others, are identical twins to Adam, even from our conception in the womb. Psalm 51:5 says, *"Behold I was brought forth in iniquity, and in sin my mother conceived me."*

No one was chosen arbitrarily, randomly, or by some divine whim.

On the contrary, God's criteria for culling and narrowing down His choices were and remain specific. It's simply this: God provided His only Son as the singular source of redemption for anyone infected with Adam's sin.

For God so loved the world that He gave His only son that whoever believes in Him should not perish but Have everlasting life. (John 3:16)

Anyone who would trust God's choice and receives His righteousness instead of offering their own righteousness, God would choose. Anyone refusing this process, God would reject.

This is why the moment you surrendered your heart to Jesus, there was a celebration in heaven. This celebration is rivaled only by that great and glorious day in which we all sit and feast with Jesus at the marriage supper of the Lamb.

And I say to you, there is more joy and rejoicing in heaven when one sinner repents than over the 99 righteous persons who have no need of repentance. (Luke 15:7)

There is great care and constant focus set upon you... You are handpicked by the Lord, officially chosen as an exclusive vessel for His own habitation.

Now everything about God contradicts all worldly knowledge and wisdom. The world seeks to only choose the strongest, the brightest, and the best, so there is inherit within each of us, a constant pressing and drive for first place (i.e., being on top).

The strongest is always placed ahead and over the smallest and weakest.

But within God's kingdom dynamics, "being weak" is where God's power is demonstrated fully and unhindered. As a matter of fact, at the slightest indication of any self-effort or human ability, God's power is reduced or even neutralized.

Please consider prayerfully these next verses:

But God has chosen foolish things of the world to shame the wise, weak things to shame the strong, lowly, and despised things, even the things which are considered as nothing to quash the things that are. (1 Corinthians 1:27–29)

Deuteronomy 7:7 says, *"For the Lord did not choose or set His affection on you, [Israel] because you were more than any other people, for you were the fewest even the least of all the nations [in every respect]."*

And finally, beloved, consider God's position on the matter.

And you who are strong ought to bear with the failings of the weak and not to please your- selves, each of us (the strong) should serve our neighbors for their good and build them up. For even Christ did not come to please himself, but for the benefit of the many. (Romans 15:1–3)

Beloved, we are a chosen generation, a royal priesthood, a Holy nation, God's own special people. proclaiming the praises of Him who called us out of darkness into His marvelous light. (1 Peter 2:9)

As always, in His love, Pastor Ken Reed

AUTHENTIC

That which is not counterfeit or copied; the original; the incorrupt; to be fully trustworthy; genuine and pure.

During my impressionable teen years, Michael Jordan was the most phenomenally gifted and exciting player in professional basketball. There were hundreds of talented young men who played in the NBA, but none were able to command the thrill and amazement of number 23, Michael Jordan.

His infamous pull-up jump shot, and his famed hang time were all astounding, but his ability to manipulate the ball seemingly at will and complete impossible shots was and, in my opinion, *remains his alone.*

He seemed on occasion to push the laws of gravity. This ability has seldom been duplicated. Many a young boy has dreamed and pretended that he was number 23. "I want to be like mike" became a mantra in all forms of advertisements. His influence has inspired several of today's most talented players.

Anything extraordinary and authentic will always inspire multiple versions and imitations of itself. This can cause identical copies or what is also known as counterfeits. It is often said that *imitation is the highest form of flattery.*

Beloved, in today's trendy and "advanced" culture, we are engulfed by a proliferation of imitations and counterfeits. So much so, we seldom experience the genuinely authentic. This hypocrisy is so effective that the pure and authentic is ofttimes rejected, being considered insensitive and offensive.

It has proven itself effective in every aspect of life. None are immune to its subtlety, from politicians pretending to care to the body of Christ where we are called into authenticity, not hypocrisy.

This present trend of feigning genuineness has crippled humanity in its ability to live purely authentic lives, which is why we are instructed in scripture to *put on the whole armor of God so that we may be enabled to stand our ground on the evil day, which can easily be every day*.

We are then instructed to put on *the belt of truth first*. (See Ephesians 6:10–18.) Truth is the core ingredient in authenticity.

The belt holds all things together. It is in knowing what's true and then mixing faith with that truth that allows you and me to live a whole and complete life in Christ Jesus.

Faith is the singular thing *without which we cannot be pleasing to God* (Hebrews 11:6), reason being every aspect of the Christian life is unattainable through any human ability or effort. It is only by means of genuine faith that we can engage God's divine nature.

Beloved, faith cannot be an imitation or a counterfeit. It must be original, genuine, and authentic. Only God can develop an original, pure, authentic faith. This is His work, not ours. *Anything produced by my own efforts is my imitation of the genuine*, but everything initiated in you by the spirit of God is perfectly original and authentically His.

Dear friends, do not be surprised at the painful trial you are suffering, as though some- thing strange were happening to you. But rejoice that you participate in the sufferings of Christ, so that you may be overjoyed when his glory is revealed. (1 Peter 4:12–13)

1 Peter 1:6–7 says, *"We greatly rejoice even though at this present time, we may have to endure all kinds of griefs in all kinds of trials. These trials come so that our faith, like gold, is purified by holy fire, producing only the purest of genuine and authentic faith."*

As always, in His love, Pastor Ken Reed

FOCUS

An adjustment in vision or concentration; developing the clarity in perception or understanding; to direct your attention or activity.

Prevalent in the consciousness of the average Western executive is the concept that true productivity is limited only by one's capacity to multitask.

Many professional and executive development programs will offer multitasking training as a key component to their educational business curricula.

This mindset is now securely positioned within most modern cultures worldwide. It is not limited to just the business environment. It is now how most of us chose to live our daily lives, *presuming being busy is being productive and obedient.*

It is God Almighty who has created you and me; He knows how we are designed to function in spirit, soul, and body. And because He has not made us to be robotic, we are free to choose any lifestyle we desire.

However, violating His perfect kingdom order in any manner will naturally result in disorder, leading us to face the consequence.

The Bible, in 1 Corinthians 6:19–20 (NIV84), clearly reminds us, "Do you not know, that your body is a temple of the Holy Spirit, who is in you, whom you have received from God? You are not your own; you were bought at a price. Therefore, honor God with your body." I am aware of the theological context of this text; however, *this context seems to have a valid application as well.*

Humanity *was never created to be or live a divided life in any form.*

If a kingdom is divided against itself that kingdom cannot stand if a house is divided against itself that house cannot stand.
(Mark 3:24)

Matthew 6:24 says, "*No one can serve two masters, he will hate one and love the others or he will be devoted to one and despise the other.*"

Even the first commandment, "Love the Lord your God, with all of your heart, soul, and mind" (Matthew 22:37), clearly shows that we are created to be single-minded and singular in our focus on God alone.

This principle is expanded upon in Matthew 6:22–23: "The eye is the lamp of the body. If your eyes are good, your whole body will be full of light. But if your eyes are bad, your whole body will be full of darkness. If then the light within you is darkness, how great is that darkness!"

Let's take a brief look at what Jesus is saying.

First of all, He is speaking about the value of prioritizing and managing your focus on the things that really matter.

The things on which you set your eyes on or focus upon most will have authority within you. This will either allow light or darkness to gain entrance and management within you. Keeping your eyes on good things will lead to fewer fleshly struggles.

But we can also see the contrast between a good singular focus and the carelessly scattered one.

James 1:7 (NIV84) says, "*Any man who is unfocused in His faith should not think he shall receive <u>anything</u> from the Lord, for he is double-minded and has become unstable (unfocused) in all of His ways.*"

There are two Greek words used in reference to the word *double-minded*. One is *dipsychos*, meaning *vacillating in opinion and purpose*, and the second is the word *schizo*. It is where we get our word *schizophrenia*, meaning *two-souled or two minds*. Anyone who suffers with this torturous ailment is faced with having two voices, thoughts, or minds *functioning in their heads at the same time*.

Beloved, let us be single-minded and clear-focused as we trust the faithfulness of God in our daily lives.

As always, in His love, Pastor Ken Reed

VOW

A solemn, unbreakable promise; a nonchanging oath; the deepest commitment possible; to swear at the risk of a curse should you fail.

Presently it is not uncommon for us to hear virtuous pledges and vows being spoken. Many consistently boast of their elevated standards of integrity and commitment; they can be overheard in every facet of our lives, from politicians, all parties included, to giant corporations who promise quality in their products and outstanding customer service, to marital relationships promising fidelity, to the police promising to "protect and serve," and to the fathers promising not to violate their own children.

Even church leaders promise before God to care for the weak and not to fleece or seduce the sheep. The list goes on and on. Few keep their vows; this present culture and world are full-on corrupt and selfish.

Psalm 15:1 asks this question: "Lord, what kind of person shall be able to abide in Your presence?" Several qualities are mentioned, but there is one that stands out—verse 4: "He who swears to his own hurt and does not change his mind."

A vow is a function for fallen humanity who cannot be trusted to keep an ordinary word. The vow tends to be a deeper or the deepest level of commitment for keeping your word. Again, vows are a human necessity for the governing of integrity.

If a man makes a vow to the Lord, or swears an oath that binds to an agreement, he shall not break his word, he shall do according to all that proceeded out of his mouth. (Numbers 30:2)

God does not ever have to make any vows; God does not speak or make any promises in varying dimensions of integrity. He faithfully keeps His word to you and me.

It is written man shall not live on bread alone, but by every word that proceeds out from the mouth of God. (Matthew 4:4)

Numbers 23:19 says, *"God is not like a man that He would Lie, nor is He born of human descent that he can change His mind, has he ever spoken and then not acted, or has He ever made a promise that He has failed to bring to pass."*

Every threatening circumstance or event confronting you and me has a genuine potential to harm us; these threats contradict God's promises of safety and protection.

Nonetheless, His words are true. It is impossible for God to lie. There is no pressure that can be placed upon God that could force Him to change His mind regarding you and me.

So, beloved, you need only to make one vow: "Set your heart on things above where Christ is seated at the right hand of the father" (Colossians 3:1).

Look to and trust His divine faithfulness to you. He has given His Holy Spirit in us as a heavenly deposit to purchase us. We are God's property.

"He is my Helper who helps me in my weaknesses." The Greek translation of this text says it this way: "The Holy Spirit take hold with me against."

Remember, God's power is being made perfect, whole, and complete inside all human weakness, not in any human strength. *For it's when I'm weak that is when I'm strong* (2 Corinthians 12:10).

As always, in His love, Pastor Ken Reed

RELINQUISH

To voluntarily cease control; to withdraw and retreat; to release possession or ownership thereof; to yield and surrender your rights.

There is within each and every one of us a hidden and deep- seated longing for love, acceptance, and authority (i.e., to be in control of the events affecting or impacting our lives).

Even those of us who persistently shun and avoid the responsibilities of being the decision makers are still, *while under the cover of apprehension and shyness, demonstrating a variant aspect of control.*

Authority or control itself is not evil. The problem is within the vessels through which it is expressed, that is, sinful and corrupt mankind (i.e., you and me).

It's like this... There was nothing wrong with the law of God for it was perfect. It originated from our perfect and loving heavenly Father. *The law only became a problem when mankind endeavored to do what it said.*

All self-effort is fleshly, flowing out from our *corrupted, sin-infected natures*. Beloved, all of our sincere attempts at obeying God's perfect laws will always end in defiling the pure and holy.

For we know that the law is spiritual; but I am unspiritual, even sold as a slave to sin. I can- not understand what I do. For what I want to do, I do not do. But what I hate to do, it seems I do naturally.

(Romans 7:14–15 NIV)

Oh, what a wretched man I am! Who will res- cue me from this body [cycle] of death? Thanks, be unto God, for we are delivered through Jesus Christ our Lord!

(Romans 7:24–25 NIV)

So how do we relinquish this self-management in our lives?

Everything starts with knowing what's true, mixing faith with that truth, and finally standing your ground in patience.

Consider, beloved, these next few scriptures within the context of our conversation.

Those who live according to the sinful nature, have their minds set on what that nature desires; In contrast to those who live in accordance with the Holy Spirit have their minds set, on what the Spirit desires. The mind of the sinful nature is death, but the mind controlled by the Spirit is life and peace. The sinful mind is always in opposition to God and is hostile towards Him. It does not submit to God's law, nor can it do so. Those controlled by the sinful nature cannot please God. (Romans 8:5–8; emphasis added)

The sinful nature can be identified by the contents of our souls, which consists of our minds (what we think), the will (personal preferences), and our emotions (all of our feelings).

Many genuine, sincere, and devoted believers have become slaves to their feelings and thoughts. This is the mind of the sinful nature.

Romans 8:9 says, "You, however, are not controlled by the sinful nature but by the Holy Spirit, if the Spirit of God lives in you" (i.e., if you are born again, then you are released from the legal dominance of your soul, and your spirit has been freed to serve the Lord). This is not a feeling but a biblical fact. *You are free whether you feel it or not.*

So, beloved, it's okay to relinquish the management of your life into the hands of "He who began the good work in you. He is faithful to complete His work" (Philippians 1:6) unto the fulfillment of His good pleasure in you.

As always, in His love, Pastor Ken Reed

RESTRAINT

To keep something or someone under control; to manage within moral limits; to practice self-discipline or moderation at all times.

All too often and with a brazen and brash voice, moral and godly boundaries are being violated. Many across all cultures have come to define freedom as a license to live without any restraints.

Alister Crowley, who is considered by some to be the father of Satanism, is quoted as saying, "Do what thou wilt shall be the whole of the law." His primary idea was this: Whatever you feel like doing, saying, seeing, having, etc. is to be yours without any limitations, personal restraint, or responsibility.

Consider the language of 2 Timothy 3:1–5:

But know this, that in the last days perilous times will come, for men will be <u>lovers of themselves</u>, lovers of money, boasters, proud blasphemers, disobedient to parents, unthankful, unholy, unloving, unforgiving, slanderers, <u>without self-control</u>, [or natural affection], brutal and despisers of the good, they will be traitors, head- strong, haughty, lovers, of pleasure rather than lovers of God, having a form of godliness but denying its power. From such people turn away!

This unrestrained focus is present within all settings and environments (e.g., husbands and wives, parents and children, employer and employee), even within the church of Jesus Christ. Just as Jesus stated in Matthew 24:7, it is nation against nation and kingdom against kingdom.

Unrestraint is all about self-gratification at the expense of some- one else.

Beloved, all unrestrained impulses are from the sinful nature. We can categorize them as we please, but at its root, it is always about me getting my own way—period.

This can include the obvious wrongdoing or even that well-intended, seemingly good thing. That urge to satisfy my own strong desire whether or not we're in a church setting still requires self-control.

At any time, I'm not restraining these urges, it is an indication that I am surrendering to some form of deception.

I will experience a momentary measure of pleasure because sin brings pleasure for a short season, but it will usually result in unfruitfulness, hurt feelings, broken trust, regret, irrevocable loss, or even death. As I've stated, restraint of any kind is usually anathema to the unconverted, but it can have an equally potent impact on the carnal, selfish, or unsub mitting believer, that is, any believer whose focus is solely on satisfying themselves first in all things.

Beloved, contrary to popular belief, Jesus's focus was not exclusively on ministry first. It was always on people. He came to redeem the lost.

Here we again apply the principles of Proverbs 3:5–7: "Trust in the Lord with all your heart, and do not presume to rely or lean upon you own understanding. In all of your ways acknowledge or look to him, and he shall direct your paths. Do not be wise in your own eyes; fear the Lord and depart from evil."

When we are living in restraint, we are saying, "Lord I am looking to you for the results. I will not push to accomplish something myself with my own strength."

In 2 Corinthians 12:19, the apostle Paul declared clearly, "It's in my weakness that God's power is experienced or made strong." So, I will always choose to restrain myself and depend on God's faithfulness in all things.

As always, in His love, Pastor Ken Reed

CURSE

To adjure a supernatural power for injury, harm, or punishment against someone or something; an evil misfortune that attends a request for harm.

The reality and option for evil is always present and lurking just below the surface in every life and situation. Evil is not a theory or a topic for religious arguments.

It is not lighthearted banter for playful experimentation; it is highly seductive and precise in its calculations. It will use any open door for entrance and management of your life. Evil will seldom if ever appear as such, for few would follow something so horrid.

For Satan will always come and masquerade himself as an angel of light [e.g., board games that promise fun-filled excitement and strange experiences or the seemingly harmless innocence of a notably celebrated fall holiday]. (2 Corinthians 11:14)

Beloved, evil has a real face, a real name, a real personality, *and a premeditated objective for your destruction.*

Satan's promise of power to control your life is his primary seductive device. Even from the beginning, his words to Adam were "And you will be like God, knowing good and evil" (Genesis 3:5) (i.e., you won't need God to plan and manage your life; you will be able to manage your life your way yourself).

The power of the curse is intoxicating to the human soul. The excitement of making a connection in the invisible dimension is intriguing and fascinating. It lures the unsuspecting into a place of darkness, terror, and legal authority for spiritual assault.

In Deuteronomy 28:1–13, God makes a covenant with Israel; He promises all blessing, all provision, all protection, and all healing (i.e., His full kingdom resources). *The only condition was obedience to His Commandments.*

He sums up the blessing in this simple statement: "I will make you the head and not the tail, you shall be above only and not beneath" (Deuteronomy 28:13).

However, in verse 14, God warns Israel if they should turn away to other gods, *they would enter the legal authority of the curse.*

The curse affects every aspect of humanity, even property and physical resources. God said *the curse would come upon them and over- come every one of them.*

There is no escape from the ruthless nature of the curse: "cursed shall you be in the city and in the country"(Deuteronomy 28:16), "the fruit of your body shall be cursed" (Deuteronomy 28:18), "when you go in, and when you come out, cursed shall you be" (Deuteronomy 28:19), "you shall be struck with disease, pestilence, confusion, depression, frustration, poverty." For the next fifty-three verses, the list of curses continues.

The apostle Paul in Romans 7:24–25 declares, "Oh wretched man that I am, who shall deliver me from this body of death? Thanks be unto God through Jesus Christ I am delivered."

Second Corinthians 5:17 says, *"If any man should surrender His life to Jesus, He shall become a non-cursed person. His old, condemned self passes away, and he becomes a brand-new creation."*

No weapon set against you will prosper, this is the inheritance of the servants of the Lord. (Isaiah 54:17)

Like a fluttering sparrow or darting swallow, a curse without cause [i.e., legal authority] shall not come upon you. (Proverbs 26:2)

And finally, Galatians 3:13–14 (emphasis added) says, "Christ has redeemed us from the curse of the Law, by becoming a curse for us. For it is written *'cursed is everyone who hangs on a tree, in so doing the blessing of Abraham has come upon those who believe.'*"

If you have given your life to Christ Jesus, continually believe that you are set free from any curse. This is who we have become in Christ Jesus.

As always, in His love, Pastor Ken Reed

GIFT

*Given willingly with no requirements of payment in any form;
to transfer or exchange ownership from one to another without
obligation or expectation of any return.*

With decadence and corruption now normalized in today's culture, the very presence of genuine authenticity has all but vanished. The notion that someone still desires to live in purity is both awk- ward and unrelatable to most, *unfortunately even in the body of Christ.*

Many do not recognize a gift, know how to receive a gift, or how to respond to one (e.g., when someone takes us to dinner, we immediately begin to think of ways to repay them for their gift, from "Let me get the tip" to "Next time it's on me.")

James 1:17 says, *"Every Good and Perfect Gift, is from God, coming down from the Father of all the heavenly Lights, He does not change or, produce any shadows."*

Generally, whenever we are exposed to purity and generosity, we tend to become suspicious and wary. We begin to think either of the following: "Wow, this is too much!" "This is too good to be true," "I'm feeling uneasy," or "What is this gift going to cost me?" And should we eventually receive the gift, immediately a subtle but deep sense of obligation to pay for the gift in some form is activated. We are always on alert to somehow repay what actually cost us nothing.

This is the experience of everyone. We all have fallen natures and corrupt hearts. Now this is especially prevalent within the Church.

> *For God so loved the world, that He gave [His most valuable asset] His only Son.* (John 3:16)

Jesus is the only gift that keeps on giving.

Beloved, no matter the depth of our sincerity, we can never do enough to merit the worth of God's gift. We have no means of paying for the gift we don't deserve.

Eternity in hell is payment for our debt of sin, but even this is not enough… *Eternity is never-ending.*

Please consider *the permanency and the effectual working of any and every gift from God.*

For it is by Grace you have been saved, through Faith, even the faith, is not from yourselves, it is the Gift of God. It is not by any of our deserving works, so that no one can boast of their own contributions. We are God's own workman- ship, we are created in Christ Jesus, to do His good works [i.e., the specific works] God has pre- pared for each of us to accomplish in advance. (Ephesians 2:8–10)

Beloved, as new creations in Christ Jesus, we are delivered from the legal authority of the kingdom of darkness and are fully released in the Son.

We are, however, still in the process of being transformed into the fullness of His likeness. *Secondly,* we are ever increasing in our understanding of the work of the Holy Spirit, *recognizing we are not the ones doing the work but the ones the work is being done in.*

So, beloved, let us guard our hearts against all the works of the flesh. Galatians 5:13-14 says, "But I say walk by the Spirit and do not surrender to the patterns of the flesh, for the natural propensities of flesh opposes the working of Holy Spirit."

If ever you are required to do something to receive a gift, it is no longer a gift. Your requirement has now become the payment for that gift. Any payment on your part neutralizes the grace of God.

As always, in His love, Pastor Ken Reed

WINTER

The coldest season of the year, the primary period of inactivity, and the time for decline and decay.

Immediately after the flood, God promised Noah, "As long as the earth remains, seedtime and harvest, cold and heat, summer and winter, day and night shall not cease" (Genesis 8:22).

God uses time to mark the beginning and the ending of every season: "And there was an *evening and a morning, day one*" (Genesis 1:5). *This is the first indication of a twenty-four-hour* cyclical nature of the planet, or we could say, <u>the entrance of time into this physical dimension</u>... *Even Jesus asked, "Are there not twelve hours in a day?" (John 11:9).*

To everything there is a season, and a time for every purpose under Heaven. (Ecclesiastes 3:1)

Time and seasons are foundational factors in everything created within the physical realm.

There is literally nothing created in this realm that does not have *a starting and an ending point.* Within those two points of existence, *God's unsurpassed wisdom and purpose are clearly displayed.*

For someone like me who spent the first ten to twelve years of his life living in the lush, hot, tropical climate of Florida, an appreciation for spring followed by summer runs deep within my seasonal veins.

When April and May begin to work their magic, the exciting evidence of new life becomes unmistakable everywhere.

Every aspect of nature seems to undergo some form of the resurrection (where all things become new).

That first fresh smell from an ocean breeze, the rhythmic pounding from the sounds of the sea, and even that tickle on your skin from the rays of a ninety-seven-degree day. How grateful I am to God for His season of summer.

Then nature begins its preparation for the season of winter. Quietly and seductively, we are lured into its process; we become intoxicated with the warm and stunning colors of fall.

Many approach this season with little to no positive anticipation. As we observe falling leaves, withered plants, and bare branches, the gradual appearance of what seems to be death becomes unshakable.

Beloved, God knows exactly the cycles and seasons needed for the earth as well as our lives.

For when the ground is frozen hard and only the lonely howl of the cold night air can be heard, all of the once beautiful trees and flowers will then be forced to grow deeper into the earth to gain their nutrients. As a result, they are then strengthened and are enabled to weather any storm. Their health and beauty will return and be on display during the following seasons of spring and summer.

Beloved, you must both know and believe that our loving Father only allows winter seasons in your life to cause growth, strengthening, and deepening of fellowship in the Holy Spirit.

Consider Hebrews 12:26–28. *God says this*:

> *Once more I will shake not only the earth, but also the Heavens, thereby removing everything that can be shaken so that all carnal*

dependencies in our lives are removed. And only the things which cannot be shaken remain [i.e., our spiritual fellowship in the Holy Spirit]. Since we have received a kingdom which cannot be shaken, let us worship God acceptably.

Lord, help us to be grateful for Your every season in our lives.

As always, in His love, Pastor Ken Reed

REST

To cease work or movement, quietness, stillness, or inactivity.

We have been unwittingly affected by many noble words and phrases that are deeply seeded into the conscience of this culture, words and phrases such as *achievement*, *accomplishment*, *attainment*, *personal pride*, and *success*, just to name a few.

These kinds of words and many more like them are necessary and highly effective for inducing and motivating the whole society into utilizing the patterns of this world.

Proverbs 14:12 reminds us "there is a way that seems right to a man, but in the end, it leads to death."

We have all been influenced and shaped, in part, by the world's platform for success, namely, "If you work hard and play by the rules, you can have the choice parts of the land as well."

God's ways and thoughts are never the worlds way, neither are His ways and thoughts as our own. (Isaiah 55:8)

Consider these next few thoughts…

In Genesis 3, as God is pronouncing the curses, He declares this: First on Adam, "Cursed is the ground because of you, through painful toil you will eat of it, all the days of your life" (Genesis 3:17).

Second, "The ground will always produce thorns and thistles for you" (Genesis 3:18).

And third, "Only by the sweat of your brow [i.e., hard work], you will eat of it" (Genesis 3:19).

The dreams and desires of the heart are often set there by God. Yet on most occasions and because of the influences of this fallen world, we *the body of Christ* tend to embrace and utilize worldly philosophies.

This thinking and process of self-reliance and personal achievement frames our sincere attempts at realizing many of the things God has set Himself to accomplish in and through us.

Beloved, "Christ has redeemed you and me, from the curse of the law, by becoming a curse for us" (Galatians 3:13).

You and I, through the sinless blood of Jesus, "have become the righteousness of God in Him" (2 Corinthians 5:21).

So, all that God has appointed for you and me is already pro- vided in His heavenly kingdom and is accessed through faith, *not hard work or any fleshly human effort.*

Praise be to the God and Father of our Lord Jesus Christ, who has blessed us [past tense] in the heavenly realms, with every spiritual blessing in Christ. (Ephesians 1:3)

Within this context, consider the simple message in Hebrews 4:1– 2: the promises of God are already provided for anyone entering God's rest, that is, we "on whom the end of the ages has come" (1 Corinthians 10:11).

We are to be *especially careful* to enter into God's rest, just as He did on the seventh day when He finished all of His work of creation.

This invitation of rest was faithfully preached to the saints of old as well as to you and me today.

However, "this message did not benefit any of them, because they who heard it, did not combine the message, with faith" (Hebrews 4:2).

Beloved, you and I must genuinely believe the Word of God and abstain from the dominate patterns of human reasoning and vain imaginations.

"We must labor to enter into God's rest," but not the labor of self-effort resulting in a sense of personal achievement.

As always, in His love, Pastor Ken Reed

DISTRACTION

The disruption of your concentration; rerouting your attention to block or diminish your focus.

Ephesians 6:151–12 says, "*Put on the full armor of God, so that you can take your stand against the devil's schemes. For our struggle is not against flesh and blood, but against, the rulers, against the authorities, against the powers of this dark world, and the spiritual forces of wicked- ness, in the heavenly realms.*"

Of all the resources in Satan's bag of schemes, strategies, and evil tactics, none are as effective against God's people as distractions.

The thing that allows distractions to be so potent a spiritual weapon against us is that it's quick, quiet, and virtually invisible.

We are vulnerable and so easily distracted, usually by something of lesser importance and value. Satanic distractions are calculated, precise, and are *tailor-made for each individual's preference*.

Some of the subtler indicators that you are being distracted are as follows: *procrastination, a lack of discipline, starting several projects at the same time, and, on a personal note, being seemingly unable to remain free of uncertainty, confusion, or harassment from a negative habit. Beloved, the list goes on.*

I can assure you that more than likely, at the root of these disappointing behaviors is the invisible culprit of distraction.

Generally, satanic distractions, being so tactical, occur at crucial moments in which your freedom and/or your victory is/are imminent. Satan, who "only comes to steal to kill and destroy" (John 10:10), employs this highly effective strategy so as to accomplish that process.

Distractions are available in a variety of appealing packaging; they can come as loud noises, clever humor, attractive and appealing individuals, etc. One of the most common ones, especially for believers, will generally occur during the ministry of God's Word. It can be *people arriving late in the service*, it can be *greeting one another at an inappropriate time*, it can be *a baby's adorable behavior*, etc.

Beloved, most distractions do not appear as such because they are cloaked in either innocence or what seems to be important.

As Jesus and his disciples were on their way, he came to a village where a woman named Martha opened her home to him. She had a sister named Mary, who sat at the Lord's feet listening to what he said, but Martha was distracted by all the preparations that had to be made [important things]. She came to Jesus and asked, Lord, don't you care that my sister has left me to do the work by myself? [She was sincere and genuine.] Tell her to help me,

Martha, Martha, the Lord answered, you are worried and upset [i.e., distracted] about many things, but only one is needful. Mary has chosen what is better, and it will not be taken away from her. (Luke 10:38–42; emphasis added)

Consider these:

No one can serve two masters. (Matthew 6:23)

We are created by God to have a singular focus. Distractions divide and split our focus.

If any of you lacks wisdom, he should ask God, who gives generously to all without finding fault, and it will be given to him. But when he asked, he must believe and not doubt [have a sin- gular focus] because he who doubts is like a wave of the sea, blown and tossed by the wind [this is the fruit of distractions]. That man should not think he will receive anything from the Lord; <u>he is a double-minded man, unstable in all he does</u>. (James 1:5–8; emphasis added)

Finally, beloved, according to 1 Peter 4:7, *"The end of all things is near. Therefore, be alert and single-minded so that you may effectively pray."*

As always, in His love, Pastor Ken Reed

SURFACE

An easily accessed outer layer; something having length and breadth but no depth.

Watching the plane disappear over the horizon was, at least for the moment, a difficult and heart-wrenching experience. The last words spoken by her fiancé was "I love you with all of my heart," and so likewise was her response to him.

Their hearts are pounding, filled with sincerity, and emotion is in that moment, defining love in its fullness.

For about six weeks, her loyalty and integrity were obvious to all. But shortly after that brief period of time, the evidence of her having only a *surface* commitment was demonstrated by betrayal and compromise.

So likewise, in this hour, just prior to the return of the Lord Jesus Christ, the depth and quality of our commitment to Him is becoming evident.

In this present cultural setting, it can be difficult sometimes to distinguish the church from the world. Consider Jesus's instruction in Matthew 7:13: "Enter through the narrow gate. For wide is the gate and broad is the road that leads to destruction, for many enter through it." And He goes on to say, "It is by their fruit, you will know them."

Fruit always takes time first to develop then secondly to ripen *so that it may become a benefit to all*.

For many whose claim is that of being Christian, there is little evidence of deeply rooted godly fruit being showcased. Their lives, appetites, and mindset are clearly framed by the philosophies of this age. *For these have only attained a surface relationship with Christ.* Jesus defines this depth of relationship in Matthew 13:5–6: "A farmer went out to sow his seed. Some fell on rocky places; where it did not have much soil, it sprang up quickly because the soil was shallow [no depth]. But when the sun came up [everyday challenges], the plants were scorched, and they withered because they had no depth of root."

In the context of our discussion, consider also Mark 11:12–14: "As they were leaving Bethany Jesus was hungry, seeing in the distance a Figtree in leaf [His church], he went to find out, if it had any fruit on it [His return]. When he reached it, he found nothing but leaves, it was not the season for figs. Then he said to the tree 'May no one ever eat fruit from you again.'" Rejected.

Beloved, the depth or quality of our commitment to Christ is not demonstrated by how much Bible knowledge we have, our church attendance, or our ability to argue the Scriptures. For even Satan can be found at this level: "He comes as an angel of light" (2 Corinthians 11:14).

Psalm 15:1–4 (emphasis added) challenges you and I to mature: "Who may dwell in your sanctuary? He whose walk is blameless, he who speaks the truth, he who has no slanderous tongue, he who loves his neighbor, and he who keeps his own word <u>even when it hurts</u>."

Beloved, unless we are continually recognizing our inability to produce the fruit ourselves and are continuously trusting the root (Jesus) to do the work, we will never develop into the person that God has purposed for us to be.

So, we are being continually warned and encouraged *to trust Him who began the work and not to depend upon our own understanding of the work of our own hands.*

Man can plant, man can water, but only God causes growth.
(1 Corinthians 3:7).

As always, in His love, Pastor Ken Reed

UNBELIEF

The absence of faith and even a refusal to believe.

All unbelief is not the same. One has an ignorant yet innocent quality, and the other has a "corrupt, rebellious quality" (i.e., "an evil heart of unbelief"). The two primary words in the New Testament translated as unbelief are *apistia* and *apeitheo*.

We all, on many occasions, experience *apista*, but the word *apeitheo* is not just passive unbelief <u>but a determined refusal to believe,</u> an <u>actual unwillingness to be persuaded.</u>

The same word is translated as unbelief *in Hebrews 3:18 and as disobedience in Hebrews 4:6.*

In Luke 1, we are granted a glimpse of unbelief (*apista*). We see a faithful and upright Zachariah struggling with unbelief; he is an example of someone who has had a lifetime of trusting God, but in this instance, he's wrestling with unbelief. His penalty for this is about a year of being unable to speak.

This behavior is contrasted in the same chapter with Mary, who is only a young and inexperienced girl. But when spoken to by the same angel with a similar message requiring faith, her response was "I don't know how this can happen but, be it unto me according to the will of God" (Luke 1:38).

We have also example of those who simply "refused" to believe. For example, those who were delivered out of Egypt died in the wilderness, never entering God's promised land because of "their dis- obedience [*apeitheo*] or their evil heart of unbelief" (Hebrews 3:12). In my opinion, unbelief is the singular, number one sin of all.

All other sins, no matter what form they may take, *flow from an unwillingness to believe God.*

This is the primary reason the Scriptures declare, "Without faith it is impossible to please God" (Hebrews11:6). And in Romans 14:23, *it clearly states that "whatsoever that does not flow from faith is sin."*

From Genesis to Revelations, those who are righteous are those who are found faithful. Those who are obedient are those who are rewarded by God. *All have one thing in common: They believed Him.* This position is paralleled with those who were considered unrighteous, unfaithful, and disobedient. They were all rewarded by *God with suffering loss, defeat, punishment, destruction, and finally death.*

Unbelief is relentless. It never gives up, it never gives in, and it is familiar and comfortable. We are all vulnerable to responding to unbelief, so this is why we must guard our hearts. Against the smallest of argument contradicting the Word of the Lord, "let God be true" (Romans 3:4).

Everything about God and His kingdom is engaged only by faith.

As always, in His love, Pastor Ken Reed

BOAST

First you must believe.

Human reasoning and our intellectual process are the natural functions of our souls. God created the soul to engage and manage this physical, natural universe. Because of Adam's sin, this realm now contradicts the authority of God's invisible kingdom.

Remember, beloved, "that which is born of the flesh is flesh, and that which is born of the Spirit is spirit" (John 3:6).

Faith in God is a continuous spiritual construct "for we walk by faith and not by sight" (2 Corinthians 5:7).

Unbelief is the ultimate expression of self-reliance, self-confidence, self-righteousness, and self-elevation. These are fathered by pride.

We must always be on the lookout for Satan's original and most effective lure to man: "And you shall be as God, knowing good and evil" (i.e., you really don't need God; you can make the decision yourself) (Genesis 3:5).

To speak with excessive pride, exaggeration, and self-satisfaction about one's achievements, possessions, or abilities.

For some, this characteristic is found in abundance, being unhindered and seemingly without any regard to humility. For others, this trait is frequently wrestled with in an effort to keep it at bay.

We all tend to recognize how ugly and repulsive this trait can be. So in most cases, we attempt to conceal it *with the use of overused clichés and restrained behaviors.*

Beloved, as believers in Christ Jesus, we are not immune to this corruption. The DNA of fallen man is contaminated and infused with this subtle poison. We are indeed "new creations in Christ Jesus; the old has gone and the new having come" (2 Corinthians 5:17). This is great news!

What this means for you and me is that Satan and his kingdom have lost its <u>legal authority</u> to govern us. *This is true, final, and unchangeable.*

However, the very nature of the devil is of one who has no regard for righteousness *or the willingness to respect that which is legal.*

I say by the grace given me, to every one of you, do not think of yourself <u>more highly</u> than you ought to think, but to think soberly because God has dealt to each one of us, the measure of faith, which He has purposed for us. (Romans 12:3; emphasis added)

Ephesians 2:8–10 says, *"For by grace you have been saved through faith, and that faith is not of yourselves; it is the gift of God. It is not from our own works or effort, unless anyone should boast about our successful efforts and accomplishments. Because our corrupt nature can only produce self-elevation and prideful boastings, for we are God's workman- ship. He created us in Christ Jesus for <u>good works</u> [i.e., the works He pre- pared for us and "specifically designed" us to fulfill]"*

To experience true freedom from all prideful boastings, we must recognize this simple truth.

Humility is not you and I pretending to be smaller or less than; *this is the definition of hypocrisy.*

My behavior may appear to be humble and gracious to you, but "men always judge by the outward appearances, God always judges by the heart" (1 Samuel 16–17).

Beloved, the only way for me to move genuinely in humility is by first acknowledging that I can't produce it myself. Genuine humility is only by a total dependency on the work of the Holy Spirit in all things for it is "not by might nor by power but by my Spirit saith the Lord" (Zechariah 4:6).

It is only when we are weak (*astheneo* in Greek, *a present tense verb*) (i.e., when we are being weak) that we are strong.

It is only in my weakness and in my inability does the power of the Holy Spirit flow. It is not in my capability or my determination that Christ is demonstrated.

Ephesians 6:10 says, "*Finally my brothers, be strong in the Lord and the in the power of his might.*"

Every godly characteristic only flows from the seed; we are only the branches on the tree. *Branches do not produce any fruit.*

The branch is where God has ordained for the fruit to be displayed.

The origin of the fruit stems only from the seed, so the only boasting that you and I should be expressing is a boasting in Him, not in ourselves. *He who began the work is the one who continues to work* (Philippians 1:6).

As always, in His love, Pastor Ken Reed

BOLD

The ability to take a risk in confidence and courage, with a strong and vivid appearance.

But you will receive Power [*dunamis* in Greek] after the Holy Spirit; comes on you, and you will be, my witnesses. in Jerusalem, in all Judea, Samaria and to the ends of the earth. (Acts 1:8; emphasis added)

There is a significant difference between being something and doing something. One suggests self-effort and personal discipline, and the other suggests *trusting in a pre-determined process.*

There exist two realms, two kingdoms, and, for the church, two possible options. One is physical, the other spiritual. One is natural, the other supernatural (i.e., *a choice from the flesh or one from the Spirit*). Because of the parallels in function present in both kingdoms, there is often a crossover in our sincere and genuine attempts in honoring the Lord. On many occasions, *human bravado, audacity, personality traits, and self-confidence* become substitutions for "godly boldness."

These traits are defined as follows: *"one who's not afraid to speak up, even to the people more powerful than they."*

The holy boldness of God's spirit is not required when these traits are present. However, on the surface, *they can appear to look and sound just like Jesus.*

Consider carefully Hebrews 4:14–16:

> *Since we have a great high priest, who has gone through the heavens, Jesus the son of God. Let us hold firmly to the faith we profess. For we do not have a high priest who is unable to sympathize with our weaknesses [astheneo in Greek; continuously being weak], But we have one who has been tempted in every way, just as we are, yet was without sin. Let us then approach the throne of grace with boldness/confidence…so that we may receive mercy and find grace to help us in our time of need.*

Beloved, *godly boldness* only flows from a direct connection to the Holy Spirit with the revelation of our authority in Christ Jesus.

Secondly, unless our bold behavior is the result and response of faith in the body and blood of Jesus, *we are just acting in bravado, being presumptuous, arrogant, and, quite frankly, annoying.*

When my boldness is self-powered, it produces a residue of pride, of self-righteousness, with that subtle hint of boasting in my accomplishment. For example: *"Well, I told him!"*

Proverbs 21:29, 31 say, *"A wicked man puts up a bold front. The horse is made ready for the day of battle [self-reliance] But victory rest with the Lord."*

Beloved, as we approach the soon return of our Lord, which is moving closer every day, the chaos and conflicts of this world will require the genuine work of the Holy Spirit.

No longer is my sincere "sleeves rolled up with a mind to work" self-effort acceptable. <u>The time of sincere flesh is coming to an end</u>. *"Oh Lord, have mercy on all of us."*

Psalm 121:3a, 7–8 says, "I will look to the hills for my help, my help comes from the Lord. *He will not let your foot slipped. He who watches over you will not slumber. The Lord* will keep you from all harm, the Lord will watch over your coming and going, both now and forevermore."

All confidence, boldness, and reassurance are seen in abundance as we meditate and grasp the authority of God's promises such as this one to you and me.

For it is only when we are "being weak" (*astheneo* in Greek) that we are being strong, "for God's power is made perfect, only in our inability not in our ability" (2 Corinthians 12:10).

As always, in His love, Pastor Ken Reed

JUSTICE

Being impartial and fair; equality; the administration of law, conforming to the principles of righteousness.

Of all the nations known throughout the earth, there are none that are generally framed by the ideals of freedom, liberty, and justice for all—except America.

And yet with all of the governance of this nation, its laws, its educational systems, its resources, and its genuinely noble intention for good, there is still ample evidence of disparity and the failure to "administrate laws conforming to the principles of righteousness."

True justice knows no color, culture, preference, or style.

Beloved, the origin of justice is not derived from any human perception of equity. We all like to portray and position ourselves as if the standards of justice and righteousness are measured by our own personal perceptions.

In almost every occasion, humanity's sense of justice has as its general theme *a perceived measurement of "equal parts"*—in other words, all being the same, receiving the same, being treated the same, etc. This particular notion of equality and justice has "fallen man" as its origin. Sadly, this ideal of liberty and justice for all will never be realized in this corrupt, sin-filled, fallen world.

Righteousness and true justice have its origin from the "Almighty God, who has no beginning and no ending."

> Psalm 89:14 (NKJV) says, *"Righteousness and justice are the foundation of your throne; mercy and truth are always before your face."* Isaiah 46:9–11 says, *"Remember this and fix it in your minds.*

Remember the former things of old, for I am God, and there is no other. I am God, and there is none like me. I declare the end from the beginning, from ancient times things that are not yet done. I say, my counsel shall stand, and I will do all that I please. Indeed, I have spoken it; I will also bring it to pass. I have purposed it, and I will also, do it."

From the fall of Adam, men have sought to govern themselves by their own sense of justice and righteousness. Well-intentioned as we all might be, this endeavor is impossible because all human conscience has been *corrupted by the knowledge of good and evil.*

Genesis 3:4–7 is the initial scene where the serpent's strategy is infecting the woman:

The serpent said to the woman, you will not surely die, for God knows that in the day you eat of it your eyes [conscience] will be opened. And you will be like God, knowing good and evil. So, when the woman saw that the tree was good for food, that it was pleasant to the eyes, and a tree desirable to make one wise [as God], she took of its fruit and ate. She also gave to her husband with her, and he ate. Then the eyes of both of them are opened and they knew that they were naked; and they sewed fig leaves together and made themselves coverings.

From then, even unto now, men have sought to establish their own perceptions (coverings) of righteousness and justice.

If it was possible for you and me to decide for us and to attain God's standard, there would be no need for Jesus to have come in the past or to return now. Beloved, in humility, please remember

God's simple statements in Isaiah 55:8–9: "For my ways are not your ways, says the Lord, neither are my thoughts. Your thoughts as high as the heavens are from the earth, so my ways are different than your ways and my thoughts different than your thoughts."

As always, in His love, Pastor Ken Reed

SUPERLATIVE

The highest kind or order; surpassing all others; that which is supreme, extreme, or exaggerated in language or style.

Many are your wonderful works, oh Lord God, and your thoughts towards us cannot be described. There is none who can compare with you. If I would try to declare your works, it would be too numerous for me. (Psalm 40:5 NKJV)

In English grammar, an adjective is a word used to modify or describe a noun. Such is the word *superlative*. In truth, this word should only be applied when used in reference to Almighty God. For without a doubt, there is none like Him.

By adding- *est* at the end of certain words, we are designating the objects as the b*est*, fast*est*, great*est*, high*est*, etc.

The second word, which is sometimes used in lieu of -*est*, is the word *most*, which can easily be applied to the Most High God.

Beloved, as new creations in Christ Jesus, we are continually exposed to Satan's tailor-made, evil presentations. These are being offered as a better option than God's best, highest, or greatest source of redemption and restoration for you and me.

We ofttimes need to be reminded of God's full and complete provisions made available to us and for us in Christ Jesus.

There are many beloved brethren who live their lives as if God's promises are to be embraced cautiously, tentatively, and with guarded restraint.

The superlative nature of God's fullness and the depth of which He has chosen to fellowship with us is frequently undermined by our limited, small, and narrow view of God's love for His children.

Consider the implications of the next verses…

> *Bless the Lord all my soul, and do not for- get all of his benefits: who forgives all your sins, who heals all your diseases, who redeems your life from the pit and crowns you with His love and compassion, who satisfies your desires with good things, so that your youth is renewed like the Eagles.* (Psalm 103:2–5)

Beloved, remember, God's Word is always about His intention, not our perception.

Truth is what God says, not what I think he says; truth is what God means and not what I think he means. (Pastor Ken Reed, 2018).

Our next superlative verse is Ephesians 3:20–21 (NKJV): Now, unto him who is able to do exceedingly, abundantly, above all that we are able to ask or imagine, according to his divine power that is at work in us. To him be glory in the church [that's you and me] and in Jesus Christ through- out all generations, forever and ever! Amen.

In Isaiah 55:8–9, there is a stated truth that never changes, even unto this day. The Lord has made this clear to me personally on more than one occasion when He reminded me that His ways are never my ways, and His thoughts are never my thoughts (Isaiah 55:8–9).

As new creations in Christ Jesus, we are born by the Holy Spirit, so we now have the capacity to come into agreement with His ways and His thoughts.

But there is a natural propensity to live independently and in contradiction to Him. There is a contrary perception and smallness that naturally occurs within each of us.

Everything about God is superlative; if we are to enter into a deeper dimension of fellowship in the Holy Spirit, we must allow for faith and humility to alter us and move us beyond our present constructs.

God always supplies everything we need in good measure, pressed down, and shaken together. *He always causes our cup to over- flow with His grace and mercy.*

As always, in His love, Pastor Ken Reed

BECOME

To begin to be a gradual change; the development in transformation; the process of coming into existence in time.

Everything has a beginning stage and a final stage. Nothing starts at the completion of its purpose or function. From creation, God designed this process as a core construct in the physical realm in which we exist.

On day three of creation, God introduces His unchangeable "seed principle": "Then God said, 'Let the earth produce seed-bearing plants, with seed in it, according to their own kind,' and it was so." (Genesis 1:11)

Every purpose, plan, and process of God is established within this perfect principle. It is within this environment that His will is initiated, developed, and fulfilled. It requires no adjustments, tweaking, or contribution of any kind from you and me.

Our only requirement is this: trusting His faithfulness in "sustaining all things by His Most powerful word" (Hebrews 1:3).

Luke 8:11 categorizes God's Word as seed. It is understood by all that the primary purpose of any seed is for the planting unto a harvest of its own kind.

There is no harvesttime without seed time first. God has established within every seed its own appointed time of harvest.

From the quickest (e.g., a radish takes twenty-five days, car- rots fifty days, spinach thirty days) to the slowest (e.g., an apple tree takes two to five years, sour cherry trees three to five years, sweet cherry trees four to seven years), *all harvesttimes are predetermined by the Lord*, not by enthusiasm, personal crisis, inspiration, deep desire, strong feelings, etc.

"My ways are not your ways, and my thoughts are not your thoughts. As high as the heaven is above the earth, so are my ways different than your ways and my thoughts different than yours," saith the Lord. (Isaiah 55:8–9)

Our struggle will always be in trusting God's evaluation, solution, and harvesttime versus *our own presumptions and conclusions of the same matter.*

Genesis 8:22 says, *"As long as the Earth remains seedtime and harvest time will never cease."*

In John 12:R24, *Jesus gives us a glimpse into the hidden dynamics of this process: "Unless a kernel of wheat [i.e., a seed] falls into the ground and dies, it will remain only a single seed, but if it dies it will produce seed for the Sower and bread for the eater."*

In short, unless a seed is sown in good soil (your heart), allowing time for death to occur (patience), there will be no harvesttime (answers to your prayer) producing more seed to be sown and the abundance of fruit for our consumption.

Even our redemption was executed via this divine process.

And the Word became flesh and made His dwelling among us, and we have seen the glory of the one and only, who came from the father full of grace and truth. (John 1:14; emphasis added)

God's Word, which is His "holy seed" that *is full of life and all-powerful*, is always at work in every context and especially within our spiritual wombs (i.e., any heart opened to it), as with the Virgin Mary who responded to the angel Gabriel by saying, "Be it unto me according to your word, oh Lord" (Luke 1:38) and nine months later *inheriting God's promise by her faith and patience* and even Peter, *a professional fisherman* having fished the sea of Galilee for years *saying to Jesus, the Living Word of God*, "We have fished all night and caught nothing; nevertheless at your word" (Luke 5:5).

Beloved, nothing is impossible for Him who believes. Please allow the seed of His word to remain in you, producing God's appointed harvest for you and through you.

As always, in His love, Pastor Ken Reed

WORTHY

Being deserving, equivalent, suitable, equal to, and comparable; being good enough.

All of the worth and value set within mankind has its origin from God. Mankind is the highest and most valuable thing ever created by God.

All of heaven and its inhabitants have a glorious presence associated with their existence, but none as glorious as Adam (i.e., man- kind). You and I are the only beings ever created in God's image and likeness. *Just like there is none like God, there is likewise none like you and me.*

Then God said, let us make man in our image, according to our likeness. Let them have dominion over the fish of the sea, over the birds of the air, and over the cattle and over every creeping thing that creeps on the earth. So, God created man in His own image; in the image of God, he created him; male and female he created them. (Genesis 1:26)

From the beginning, man was authorized by God to be in His presence and in fellowship with Him then to exercise God's authority and governance over all created things.

God clothed His creation in a "glorious covering" tailor-made just for them. This provided their sense of worthiness by being in fellowship with God, free from shame and condemnation.

But the moment Adam sinned, he experienced the loss of that glorious covering and with it, any sense of worthiness from being in fellowship with the holy God.

Genesis 3:7–10 says, "Then the eyes of both of them were opened and they knew they were naked; so, they sewed fig leaves together and <u>made themselves coverings</u>. Then they heard the sound of the Lord God walking in the garden in the cool of the day, and Adam and his wife hid from the presence of the Lord God among the trees of the garden. The Lord called to Adam and said, where are you? And Adam said I heard your voice in the garden, <u>and I was afraid because I was naked; so, I hid</u>" (emphasis added).

The NT word for *worthy* is the *Greek* word *axios*. *Axios has a unique origin; it was the word used in business for establishing a balanced weight or measurement.*

When business was being conducted, the payment was usually weighed (i.e., thirty pieces of silver, "the price of a slave," had a particular weight associated to it).

So, if you did not have thirty pieces but had silver equivalent to that weight, it was considered equal to the full weight and payment, deserving and of matched value. *Your offer would be accepted.*

Beloved, there is only one who is worthy, *fully weighted, comparable, deserving, equivalent, and good enough*. And that, of course, is Jesus. *Salvation is by no other name than Jesus (Acts 4:12).*

At that name, every knee shall bow, of <u>things in heaven of things in the earth, and of things</u> under <u>the earth</u>. [Please note that in Christ Jesus, the original realm of God's authority for man's governance is fully restored.] (Philippians 2:10)

There is no sincere effort or sacrifice we can offer or add to the whole and perfect offering of Jesus's body and blood.

You can always fully trust and wholly depend upon the full weight and full value of Jesus Christ. You and I can never offer to God anything of worth. However, we now have full value and worth fully restored in Jesus Christ. So, by continuously trusting the worthiness of Jesus, God will always accept His payment for my sin.

So, beloved, let us in all humility and acknowledged weakness, trust the Lord with all of our hearts, never relying upon anything of ourselves. *And you will know the hand of the Lord moving on your behalf.*

As always, in His love, Pastor Ken Reed

CREATE

To bring into existence; to originate; to make something out of nothing.

In the beginning, God created the heavens and the earth. (Genesis 1:1)

This verse goes on to say, "The earth was formless and empty" (Genesis 1:2), and then, "God said" (Genesis 1:3).

The ability to create can only be found within the Almighty God. Hebrews 11:3 says, "It is only by faith that we understand, that the universe was formed at God's command, so that what is seen was not made/created, out of what was visible" (i.e., God did not use preexisting materials to create the universe; He made all things out of nothing).

On the contrary, there is no creative ability in Satan, no capacity to originate or bring anything into existence. He only manipulates and restructures God's intended natural order for all things.

Even his own existence is a corruption of God's intended order. God created Lucifer to be a "bright shining star," but Satan, out of his pride, corrupted himself, altering God's order and divine purpose. As you and I live from day to day, we soon recognize our inability to bring to pass anything significant. (*Though we continually try as if we can.*)

This is why no human effort or ability is ever acceptable to God.

Human effort, in spite of heartfelt sincerity, can only produce natural or less than natural levels of result.

Man cannot, by himself, fly, heal the common cold, raise the dead, etc. Though human efforts are admirable and appreciated by others, they can never result in the fullness of God's purpose.

God's standard is not "our best or sincerest efforts." God's standard is always wholeness and perfection.

Because of God's love for you and me, He has by His grace set in us His kingdom. In addition, *He has left us a deposit in the form of the Holy Spirit*, who is to govern God's kingdom within our hearts.

In the Bible, 1 John 4:4 (emphasis added) says, "You are of God, little children, and have overcome the world; because Greater is He who is in you, than he who is in the world."

God has provided His spirit in you and me; His workings are off the scale of any human effort. Beloved, as new creations in Christ Jesus, we are created, tailor-made, as it were, as vessels for the works of the Holy Spirit.

God's intention is for the accomplishment of His *perfect will and purpose.*

Ephesians 3:10 says, "His intent was that now, through the church [that's you and me], the manifold wisdom of God, should be made known, to all the rulers and authorities in the heavenly realms."

Always remember, beloved, you and I are created to serve God's purpose, *not to live a life as we imagine it to be.*

Philippians 1:6 says, "It is God who began a good work in you. He is the one who faithfully continues working until its completion in Christ Jesus."

Philippians 2:13 also says, "For it is God who works in you both to will and to do according to His good pleasure/purpose."

So, as we move from day to day, all of our efforts are to be applied to "entering God's rest," "for anyone who has entered God's rest <u>has ceased from his own work/efforts</u>" (Hebrews 4:9–11).

As always, in His love, Pastor Ken Reed

INSTANT

An immediate moment; a short space of time; having an urgent and pressing longing for now.

Everything governing our existence is framed by God's planning and His perfect timing. It is clear in Scripture that God *knows the end of everything right from the beginning* (Isaiah 46:10).

Isaiah 65:24 says, "It will also come to pass, that before they call, I will answer them, and while they are still speaking, I will hear." In Genesis 1:3, we see that the first thing God created was light.

There are two points of interest. First, *creation only occurs as a result of God speaking*. Second, we see the introduction of time: "And there were an evening and a morning, the first day" (Genesis 1:5).

It is introduced here *what we now know to be scientifically accurate.* The earth rotates at a speed of approximately 1,000 mph, and the earth has a circumference of approximately 25,000 miles, which gives us on average a twenty-four-hour rotation, *an evening and a morning* (i.e., twelve hours of the day and twelve hours of the night). *One additional day is formed from the extra mileage and time, which is why we have a leap year.*

Jesus confirms this in John 11:9–10: "Are there not twelve hours of daylight? A man who walks by day will not stumble, for he sees by this world's light, it is when he walks by night that he stumbles, for he has no light." You may say, "This is all interesting, Pastor Ken, but so what?"

My point is this… We who "love the Lord" have a constant internal longing to experience His purpose, presence, and power *in a real and tangible way*. The yearning itself is admirable; it is a side effect of the Holy Spirit living in us.

So, our personal longings for God's presence is not the issue. It is how we think about experiencing it. We all tend to forget that "it is God who created and made us" (Psalm 100:3).

Only truth releases us from any management and/or influence of the devil. His only effective weapon against God's people is the lie, of which he is the originator. He is the perfect liar; he is almost irresistible. Our tactical defense is a threefold process: first, knowing the truth, second, mixing faith with that truth, and third, standing our ground in that truth (i.e., *patiently trusting the faithfulness of God in all matters*).

Be aware of the fallacy of immediacy.

Beloved, if God's intention for us were that everything is to be instantaneous, there would be little need for faith and patience "by which we inherit the promises of God" (Hebrews 6:12).

Scripture makes clear and elevates the position of "faith" as we endeavor to engage Father God and the dynamics of His kingdom.

Can you glimpse God's intention for our development in these next verses?

As always, in His love, Pastor Ken Reed

SHAKEN

Put on the whole armor of God, so that you may be able to stand against the wiles of the devil. We do not wrestle against flesh and blood [natural things], but against principalities, and powers. The rulers of this dark age and their spiritual hosts of wickedness in heavenly places. And having done all to stand, stand with your loins girded about with the belt of truth. (Ephesians 6:11–14)

For without faith, it is impossible to please God.
(Hebrews 11:6)

And 1 Peter 1:6–7 says, "*For a little while, you may have to suffer grief in all kinds of trials. These trials come so that your faith is proven to be genuine and of greater worth than pure gold, which will perish even though it is refined by fire. Genuine faith results in, glory and honor when Jesus Christ is revealed.*"

Faith must be tested, so as to be proven as genuine.

And so, beloved, "do not throw away your confidence. It will be richly rewarded. You need to persevere so that when you have passed the test, you will receive the promise of God" (Hebrews 10:35–36).

Quick, jerky movements in any direction; sudden and abrupt motions; to vibrate, to tremble, or to be disturbed.

The classic line made popular in almost every *James Bond* film was smartly delivered as "Shaken, not stirred," the implication being that the shaking process would result in something unique and *special*.

There are a number of naturally occurring shaking events that can have an impact on and in our daily lives. The most dramatic and obvious is the earthquake.

Consider the cause of an earthquake. First, it begins with a slow buildup of <u>pressure</u>, which creates *stress points* on the tectonic plates. This process leads to a sudden shift of those plates, *resulting in violent and destructive shaking.*

Shaking can and does occur within a wide assortment of con- texts in an individual's life. On most occasions, it is unrecognized or appreciated as something valuable, *a necessary experience.*

But for you and me who are now new creations in Christ Jesus, there is to be an awareness and an eagerness to welcome the attitude of 1 Corinthians 6:19–20 (emphasis added): "Do you not know that your, body is the temple of the Holy Spirit, who lives in you, and whom you have received from God? <u>You are not your own; you were bought at a price</u>, therefore honor God with your body."

In short, brethren, our lives are no longer for the satisfying of our own longings or desires but for the completion and expression of God's unique design for you and me.

We are like sacred buildings still under construction; we are not in our completed state as of this moment.

He who has begun His good work in you, is still at work in you and me, he will faithfully continue His construction process until it is completed. (Philippians 1:6 NIV84)

Now, beloved, please *carefully consider these next verses…* See to it brethren, that you do not refuse him who speaks. For if they [old covenant saints] did not escape when they refused him [Moses and the law] who warned them on the earth, how much less will we if we turn away from Him who warns us from heaven [Jesus Christ]?

At that time, God's voice shook the earth [at Mount Sinai], but now [today] God has promised "Once more I will shake not only the earth but also the heavens." Now the words "once more" indicate that God is removing everything that can be shaken (i.e., all created or natural things). So that the things which cannot be shaken may remain. (Thereby becoming the only things of value in our lives.)

Now because we in Christ Jesus have received a Kingdom that cannot be shaken, let us be thankful, and worship God whole-heartedly, with reverence and in awe. For our God is a consuming fire. (Hebrews 12:25–29)

Because of God's great love for His children, He by the Holy Spirit manages our exposure to every occasion of shaking. He is careful to ensure that *every situation whether good or bad is limited and is working only for our good (Romans 8:28).*

Beloved, as we are being entrenched more deeply into the final days, *please* allow God's perfect work to continue to function beyond the depth of your own understanding, *into the invisible realm of trusting Him with all of your heart.*

As always, in His love, Pastor Ken Reed

ANTICIPATION

An emotion involving pleasure or anxiety when considering or awaiting an expected event; the act of looking forward.

As the young and newly wedded couple stroll through the aisles of infant wear in a large department store, their hearts are full of *anticipation*.

The wife's face is now beaming with a glow of joy and excitement since becoming conscious of a life now active within her womb. She anticipates that in the near future, *God will graciously allow her to give birth to her lifelong dream and desire*.

The husband, likewise, exudes an air of prowess as he strokes his hands over the threads of a football. And in quiet *anticipation*, he ponders momentarily the touchdown pass of a future big game.

Now both people are moving in the place of spiritual law, which is set within each of us by our loving, heavenly Father.

Jeremiah 29:11–14a (NKJV) says, "*For I know the plans I have for you declares the Lord, plans for good and not for evil, to give you a hope and a future. Then you will call upon me and pray to me, and I will hear you. And you will seek me and find me, when you search for me, with all of your heart. I will be found by you, says the Lord, and I will bring you back from your captivity. I will gather you from all the nations, and from all the places where I have driven you, says the Lord." Jeremiah 32:27 declares this unchanging word:* "Behold, I am the Lord, the God of all flesh. Is there anything too hard for me?"

Within every human being, there is an inborn, created witness of the spirit of God. It is especially activated within you and me as children of God. *We all know that there is a God.*

For the heavens declare the glory of the Lord, and the skies proclaim the work of his hands, Day after day they pour forth speech, and night after night they reveal knowledge. (Psalm 19:1–2 NIV84)

Now, beloved, you and I, just like our young couple, *have received a promise and can now live in a place of positive anticipation.*

There is, however, a distinct difference between living in anticipation and expectation. They are not the same.

Anticipation is the looking forward in hopefulness to what is coming. The main idea is in resting, in the assurance, that it will be good regardless of what form it takes. *This can also be defined as faith.*

Expectation, though similar, can have a more imaginary reality of the future. This imagined reality can be limited to one's personal ability, and focused on things that are untrue, which contradicts *"the purpose and plans God has for you."*

God loves us and "has given to us exceedingly great and precious promises, that by these we might inherit the Kingdom" (2 Peter 1:4).

Only as you and I live daily with a singular focus can we truly anticipate *the fulfillment of such promises.*

Beloved, by trusting God in every situation, we are anticipating His intervention at any moment. And because we know He loves us; we have great confidence and hope in His faithfulness. And lastly, "he who began the good work in you is continuously at work in you" (Philippians 1:6), so every situation, good or bad, is ultimately working for our good.

As always, in His love, Pastor Ken Reed

CARELESS

Inattentive, unconcern, insufficient thought, and neglect.

This word is usually used as a description of someone whose decisions display a consistent pattern of irregularity and instability. These decisions will often result in a series of harmful experiences, some of which having fatal potential *to themselves and others*.

Immediately, we can envision various scenarios in which *carelessness* can have fatal consequences for you and others.

Just imagine a careless surgeon, one with no focus on details, or the carelessness in the cockpit of the jumbo jet of which you are a passenger.

These are obvious extremes; however, *carelessness in any scenario has a great potential for injury or the loss of life.* And lastly, imagine a father holding his newborn baby for the first time and, because of *carelessness*, dropping her.

So, what is one of the primary causes of *carelessness*?

First of all, no one is perfect in any dimension, so accidents, mishaps, mistakes, etc. *will always be a part of our human experience.* So, let's make a clear distinction *between the nature of imperfection and the characteristic of carelessness.*

Let's start with this simple distinction: One is *unavoidable* and inherent within all humanity (imperfection). The other has the potential of being *preventable* on every occasion (carelessness).

Now this next thought is a general assessment; it is not exclusive by any means. There are obviously other ingredients that have the potential for supporting the expression of carelessness in my life and yours.

I start with a presumption. *There is always the <u>presumption</u> that we are okay and that we can manage the present experience (i.e., I've got it all under my control / I already know, so I can depend on what I know [i.e., my ability]).*

Beloved, this is especially prevalent in we who are new creations in Christ Jesus.

The presumption is one of the most lethal weapons Satan employs against you and me. This dynamic of presumption is so subtle that it is almost imperceptible *as it wreaks havoc within us.*

Presumption draws most of its strength from our struggle with pride and our own self-perception. *On the contrary, humility is God's instrument and the only thing that can neutralize and completely disarm presumption.*

As we walk with Jesus, opportunities for an invasion of carelessness is ever present.

It is only as we consider the possibility of us not being enough (humility) and that we might be wrong can we begin to minimize the potential for carelessness. *So, let's wait upon the Lord a little longer.*

And particularly now as we begin the "final approach" *to the return of our Savior Jesus,* take to heart the present warning signs.

Brethren, *presumption and carelessness* are distractions you and I can no longer afford to spend time recovering from.

And do this, understanding the present time: the hour has already come for you to wake up from your slumber because our salvation is nearer now than when we first believed the night is nearly over; the day is almost here so let us put aside the deeds of darkness, and put on the armor of light. (Romans 13:11–12)

As always, in His love, Pastor Ken Reed

CLARITY

Transparency, precision, or lucidity in all perception and understanding; to be free of any ambiguity or shadows.

Of all the unique and astounding abilities functioning within each of us, none are as critical as our capacity for *communication and understanding.*

We recognize the truthfulness of this statement in a flash because *even in this moment, we are engaged in the process of* <u>communicating and understanding.</u>

We are the only beings created in the image and likeness of God. Even God's glorious angelic hosts are not created in His image. We are created in three parts: first, as spirit beings, second, we have souls, and third, God housed these in a physical body.

All communication and understanding are developed within the construct of the soul, consisting of <u>the mind,</u> (intellectual ability) <u>the will,</u> (our capacity for choice and decision), and <u>our emotions</u> (all feelings, passions, and desires).

We all send and receive information through the function of the soul. We all need a measure of clarity before taking any action. Whenever there is a lack of clarity, we consider that action risky and unwise, we will usually hesitate or even refuse to engage in it.

Our minds require enough clear information so that we can evaluate it as reasonable, draw conclusions, then act. This is the natural order for all communication and understanding.

Anything lacking this kind of clarity is normally not appealing to any of us. Few of us are drawn to abstract thought. Few of us find ambiguity, especially in critical situations, appealing. In most cases, we become frustrated in the absence of intellectual clarity. Understanding provides that sense of confidence we require in the decision-making process. But God declares, "My ways are not your ways. And my thoughts are not your thoughts" (Isaiah 55:8).

Briefly, all of our words consist of thoughts and ideas. Afterward, we all tend to labor, to add substance to our ideas.

But God's words and His thoughts "are full of life and all-powerful" (Hebrews 4:12).

God's words can create themselves and require no assistance.

Remember the former things, those of long ago; I am God, and there is no other; I am God, and there is none like me. I make known the end from the beginning, from ancient times, what is still to come. I say, my purpose will stand, and I will do all that I please. What I have said, that will I bring about; what I have planned, that will I do. (Isaiah 46:9–11)

As new creations in Christ Jesus, you and I are restored to *full spiritual fellowship with God.*

Our ability for hearing His voice in all clarity is online.

"But Pastor Ken, why do I still struggle to hear God's voice?"

We are so adept in the use of our souls for communication and understanding that we subconsciously use the same "physical mechanism" (our souls) *in an attempt to engage God's spiritual process.*

It is in an environment of stillness and quietness that hearing His voice occurs. God continuously speaks to us twenty-four hours a day, but we are so attuned to giving our attention to the loud, dramatic shouts of our emotions that we allow these voices to cloud the whispers of the Holy Spirit.

Be still and know that I am God; I will be exalted among the nations. (Psalm 46:10)

God's people, being overwhelmed with the noises of pharaohs chariots and the clamor of their own fear, could not hear the voice of God.

Beloved, our Father only speaks in perfect clarity.

He who has an ear to hear, let him hear. (Matthew 11:15)

And Moses said, "Do not be afraid, stand still and you will see the deliverance of the Lord, the enemy you see today, you will never see again." (Exodus 14:13)

As always, in His love, Pastor Ken Reed

GUIDANCE

*Critical instruction in resolving specific problems or providing
continual direction in the maintenance of life.*

What is the purpose of guidance? And if it is so vitally crucial to
our existence, why does it seem to be so tricky in recognizing it,
accepting it, and engaging in it?

The nature of God's guidance reveals His omniscience (i.e., His
foresight and great wisdom [knowing the end from the beginning]).

Because God knows the end from the beginning, He took great care
to set in place *a process for the instruction of His children.*

Nothing was left to chance. In fact, the simplicity of its complexity
and the complexity of its simplicity highlights God's astounding
wisdom and validates that He alone is God and there is none like
him.

Adam was created to have fellowship with the Lord, but as new
creations in Christ Jesus, you and I are recreated. Having the Lord
and His Kingdom established within us, we live and breathe His
presence.

*God has not made communication with Him difficult, complex, or
mysterious, beloved. We have done that ourselves!*

We have elevated our own experiences, either good or bad, and the misrepresentations of well-meaning brethren, all of which being assisted by the father of the lie: Satan.

We make verses such as "As many as are led by the Spirit of God" (Romans 8:14) more complex than God intended it to be.

Everything about fellowship in the Holy Spirit has everything to do with God's holy Word. The Holy Spirit never takes any action that is not framed by word from the mouth of God.

Much of our confusion stems from our devaluing this truth then overvaluing that. Somehow *the guidance and instruction of the Holy Spirit will mysteriously float into our conscience independent of scripture.*

We have made "fellowship in the Holy Spirit" vague, ambiguous, imprecise, and something only "special people" cab discerns.

This is simply untrue. Please carefully consider God's heart in prioritizing our relationship to His Word in these few samplings of Scripture.

Your word is a lamp to my feet and a light to my path. (Psalm 119:105)

Without the light of God's Word as our central focus, we are easily distracted and trip over the debris placed in our path by the enemy of our souls. Stumbling blocks are designed to keep you and me off balance so that we easily trip and eventually fall.

Psalm 119:111 says, *"Your word I have hidden in my heart that I might not sin against you."*

Distractions easily affect your eyes and focus so that you look away. They draw your attention to themselves and your own understanding instead of God.

For the word of the Lord is full of life and all-powerful, and sharper than many two-edged swords, it penetrates even to separating the soul from the spirit, the joints, and marrow, it judges the thoughts and intentions of the heart. (Hebrews 4:12)

For it is written, man shall not live on bread alone, but by every word that proceeds from the mouth of God. (Matthew 4:4)

Beloved, keep your heart fixed on this simple truth: *God loves you.* Open His holy Scripture, quiet your heart, and ask the Holy Spirit to "provide wisdom and revelation in the knowledge of him" (Ephesians 1:17), and you will experience God's grace extended to you by the *all-powerful life of the Holy Spirit in God's Word.*

As always, in His love, Pastor Ken Reed

PREPARATION

To make ready beforehand; the action taken in advance of an event or an undertaking.

It is often said that *plans fail because those involved failed to plan.* Beloved, everything from your birth to your death requires some form of preparation. Before a child comes from a mother's womb, the body, all by itself, begins the process of preparing for the development of new life.

Every moment from inception to the actual moment of birth, the body continues in the process of preparing for the event.

Preparation is no doubt one of the most, *if not the most, vitally important and mandatory actions we must take during our lifetime.*

No one can live a meaningful life without consciously and constantly making the appropriate preparations.

One of the major side effects of Adam's sin is this: *Nothing lasts, and no one lives forever.*

Of the two trees in the garden of Eden was the tree of eternal life. God graciously removed fallen man from the garden before he could attempt to eat of that tree as well and *remain forever in his corrupt, fallen state of sin and death.*

<u>So as a result, nothing in this realm last forever</u>, not the doctors who care for us, or the dedicated healthy regiments of organic diets and exercise.

Even the medicines prescribed to help us stay alive have an expiration date.

There is nothing worse than facing the inevitable without having made in advance proper preparation.

> *It is appointed for men to die once and after this their judgment, so Christ was sacrificed once to take away the sin of many; and he will appear a second time not to bear sin, but to bring salvation to those who are waiting for him [i.e., those who are prepared].*
> (Hebrews 9:27–28)

In Christ Jesus, we know that our full life begins when this present life ends. *And technically, in Christ we have already entered into that life* for as believers, we do not die. *We simply fall asleep.*

> *Oh, death where is your sting? Oh, grave where is your victory?*
> (1 Corinthians 15:55–57)

In John 14:1–10 (emphasis added), Jesus says, "Let not your heart be troubled. If you believe in God, you must believe also in me because in my father's house are many mansions. If this was not so, I would've told you; I am going to <u>prepare</u> a place for you. And as I go to <u>prepare</u> that place, I will come again and receive you to myself so that where I am, there you may be also."

Jesus also says, "No one can come to the Father except through me" (John 14:6). In other words, <u>no one can come unprepared</u>.

Finally, beloved, we must embrace this fact as being our most important preparation in life.

That is, through faith in God's Son Jesus Christ, *we do not have to reinvent the wheel or work really hard to get prepared.* <u>God finished His work in Jesus at Calvary</u>!

We simply in faith and humility must acknowledge and continually trust His love and faithfulness.

For He who began the work in you, faithfully continues it, until its completion. (Philippians 1:6)

It is through this construct that we become and remain permanently prepared.

For the just shall live by faith...from the start to the finish. (Romans 1:17)

As always, in His love, Pastor Ken Reed

SHADOW

A dark area or surface produced when a partial source of light is obstructed; a silhouette formed by the absence of light.

Shadows are our common and constant companion. They are so common that we seldom, if ever, stop to grant them our momentary attention or associate any value with them.

They are understood as simply a reflection of something genuine, not the reality itself but only a vague and abstract form of it.

Under the Old Covenant, all encounters with Yahweh, from Moses to Jesus, were understood through the use of types and shadows. They spoke of the reality of things that were yet to come.

As believers in Christ Jesus, there is a present reality that was nonexistent under the law and the commandments (i.e., the Old Covenant).

The people's confidence in God was that of a God who was always nearby.

Psalm 57:1 says, *"Be merciful to me Oh God, for my soul trusts in you in the shadow of your wings, I will take refuge until these calamities pass."*

He who dwells in the secret place of the Most High, shall abide <u>under the shadow</u> of the almighty [El Shaddai]. (Psalm 91:1)

Beloved, being "under the shadow" versus being "in Christ Jesus" are two completely different dimensions of fellowship with the Lord.

The resurrection of Jesus ended all of God's use of types and shadows.

Hebrews 10:1a (NIV84) says, "*The Law is only a shadow of the good things that are coming, not the realities or the image themselves.*"

Now I'm sure that we can all agree that a shadow of any kind is not the reality. The reality is nearby, but the reality and the shadow are two distinct forms.

One is real, having substance and depth. The other is void of tangible substance and is technically *nonexistent*.

Do not live your life in the shadows. We frequently do so with- out being consciously aware of our actions.

It usually takes the form of sincere self-effort. Beloved, all self-efforts are works of the flesh.

Now this next thought is always difficult for most of us to receive, <u>but it is true nonetheless</u>...

Doing our best is never good enough. God can only accept perfection, which is why He only accepts that which is provided by Christ Jesus Himself.

If doing your best in all sincerity was God's only requirement, there would've been no need for Jesus to come, suffer, and die for us. <u>God would've</u> said, "No problem. Do your best, and that will satisfy My criteria of wholeness, righteousness, and perfection."

Do not be deceived, my beloved brethren, every good and perfect gift comes down from above from the Father Of Lights, in whom there is no variation or any shadow that comes from Him turning.
(James 1:16–17)

It is said scientifically that light travels in a straight line and that shadows are created when light is forced to bend or shift in any direction. Our loving, heavenly Father is never going to turn His face away from you and me. His permanent posture toward us in Christ Jesus is "I will never leave you or forsake you even until the end of the age" (Hebrews 13:5).

Remember, beloved, we can attempt to live from the emptiness of shadows or by genuine faith in God's abundance for us in Christ Jesus.

As always, in His love for you, Pastor Ken Reed

STRIVE

To struggle or fight vigorously; to devote serious and sustained effort; to contend in opposition to; to make a great and tenacious effort.

The word *strive*, especially in the Old Covenant, is translated from several different Hebrew words (e.g., *reeb*, *saw-raw*, *shebeth*, *ra'yon*, just to name a few).

However, at the core, their meanings are closely related. With only context, one can make minor and nuanced distinctions in their usage.

All of our understanding as Christians should be considered in an end-time context. So please allow this word *strive* or "the act of striving" to serve as a reminder and a warning to you and me "on whom the end of the age has come" (1 Corinthians 10:11).

The first time the word is used in Scripture is by God just prior to the flood at one of the most sinful occasions in human history.

Fallen angelic beings, having left their assigned positions, were roaming rampantly throughout the earth and engaging in abominable physical relations with the daughters of men.

Genesis 6:3 says, "My Spirit shall not strive with mankind for- ever, yet his days shall be 120 years." It goes on to say *that God was disappointed that He had ever created man and that evil was in the hearts of men continually.*

And so, after striving for a specific period of time, God allows the flood (i.e., the destruction of all humanity from the face of the earth). *His time of striving with the men of that day had come to an end. This is a warning for you and me!* Jacob, from his mother's womb, was a wrestler. It seemed he was always wrestling for the position of first place, seeking the blessing and advantages associated with that position.

> *There were twin boys in Rebekah's womb, Esau came out first, after this his brother came out grasping at his heel, so he was named Jacob.* (Genesis 25:26)

Jacob epitomizes a lifetime of grasping for position in an attempt to assure his own best interests are served.

But hear God's warning!

> *My Spirit shall not always strive with man.* (Genesis 6:3)

In Genesis 32, Jacob is essentially running for his life, and the Lord allowed Jacob to come to an isolated and secluded place.

Then Jacob was left alone, and a Man wrestled with him until the breaking of the day. and when he saw he did not prevail against him; He touched the socket of his hip. and Jacob's hip was out of Joint, as he wrestled with Him. And He said let me go, for the day breaks [your time for wrestling with God is finished], but Jacob said, "I will not let you go until you bless me." … "What is your name?" … "Jacob." … "Your name shall no longer be Jacob, but Israel." (Genesis 32:32–28)

There are several valuable lessons we can extract from this episode, but please consider this: Jacob was wrestling with the will of God, *perhaps just like you and me.*

Please note: His wrestling resulted in two dramatic changes.

First, God changed his identity from a grasper (Jacob) to one "beloved of God" (Israel). Second, God changed the way Jacob walked; *for the rest of his life, he no longer walked with a self-confident strut but a fragile limp and in need of assistance.*

Beloved, do you really need to have your hip dislocated by the Lord, *or are you willing to just stop the wrestling with Him?*

Trust the Lord with all of your heart and stop relying and depending on your own strength/understanding (Proverbs 3:5).

As always, in His love, Pastor Ken Reed

EXPERIENCE

The knowledge or understanding formed from an action or an encounter, the resulting impact from exposure to a series of happenings.

Previous experience is generally a highly prized commodity in every environment. The value of such cannot be overrated. It offers the immediate assistance of safety, protection, efficiency, skill, and time-saving expertise. Experience allows for an accelerated increase of productivity and accomplishment in all categories and endeavors. There is no wonder as to why in most critical positions of authority and leadership, the primary requirement is experience. As a matter of fact, the request will often say "experienced only."

One of the things allowing someone to become the best in their field is experience. Someone could easily have an extraordinarily high level of academic theory with no practical experience.

Seven years of surgical experience is generally valued higher than ten years of sterling academic prowess.

However, with all of the accolades and benefits of human experiences, none are of a greater value than the realization and the experience of the dynamic entrance of God's kingdom in your life. This is only accomplished by the simplicity of trusting the finished work of Jesus Christ.

Beloved, no one ever becomes professional or fully experienced in the supernatural process of faith. We are ever "growing in the grace and the knowledge of the Lord Jesus Christ" (2 Peter 3:18).

The work of God in you and me is a lifetime project: "He who has begun this work continues it, until the day of Jesus' return" (Philippians 1:6).

However, many a sincere believer is dominated by their past experiences, either good or bad. This is the result of self-focus.

Jesus declared in Mathew 4:4 that "all of humanity should live not only by physical experiences but by every word coming out of the Father's mouth." His words are to become the final authority we live by.

Regrettably, God's Word, for many, has become secondary to their personal experiences, level of education, practical concepts, and reasoning.

The prioritized function of faith is always lost or diminished when reasoning or experience, either positive or negative, are elevated above the authority of God's spoken Word.

Lamentations 3:37–38 emphatically states, *"Who can speak, and have it happen if God has not commanded it, is it not from the mouth of the Lord that both good things and bad things come?"*

Beloved, do not allow yourself to become one who permits the contradictions produced by their experiences to have expression.

This is the definition of an immature, carnal, and soulish life. It lacks the biblical comprehension that is to be mixed with faith and patience so as to inherit the divine promises.

It is impossible for God to be in error or lie. With that said… I am what God says I am and have what He has declared for me, for I can do all things but only through Christ whose strength I use (Philippians 4:13).

As always, in His love, Pastor Ken Reed

CHANGE

To alter; to modify; to make different; to substitute; to replace with something else, implying an improvement.

Solomon, the wisest man in the world, stated in Ecclesiastes 1:9, "There is nothing new under the sun."

Centuries later the French writer Jean-Baptiste Alphonse coined an interpretation of this text with his now-famous quote "The more things change, the more they remained the same."

Sometimes change is authentic and impactful. At other times, it's only as Shakespeare's comedy, *Much Ado About Nothing*.

As believers and receivers in Christ Jesus, we have been changed from an old, disconnected, and dead person born infected and under the management of "the god of the world" into a brand-new creation, even unto the righteousness of God Himself.

> *Through God's perfect love for us, we can have absolute confidence in that day of judgment. Because as he is [Jesus presently], so are we, even in this world.* (1 John 4:17 NASB)

Beloved, think about the implications of Romans 6:6–7 (NIV84): "For we know that our old self was crucified with Christ so that the body ruled by sin, might be done away with [i.e., put to death].

Therefore, we are no longer slaves [*doulos*] to sin because anyone who has died has been freed from the authority and control of their sinful past."

Because Jesus's work was a final work (i.e., "It is finished" [John 19:30]), we are forever changed, *even seated with Christ Jesus, at the right hand of God.*

However, because we are created to function in two dimensions, the spiritual and the physical, we are complete in one dimension (spiritual) and being completed in the other (physical).

So, though we are changed, we are still changing.

> *He who has begun the good work [i.e., the finished work] is continuing it unto its full development and expression in Christ Jesus.* (Philippians 1:6)

In the present political climate, our nation is being bombarded with rhetoric around the idea of change. The inference is that the old direction is the cause of all of the nation's struggles. And unless we change to this "new direction," there can be no restoration of national order or equality.

It is always articulated in carefully crafted and suggestive language loaded with all the charm of which the best dreams are made of. Unfortunately, all of its foundations are rooted in *self-interest, human potential, and outright self-worship.*

Psalm 127:1 says, "Unless the Lord builds the house [i.e., makes the changes], those who would make plans or changes will labor in vain [i.e., all of their efforts are useless]."

This truth has genuine application in any context whether in or out of the body of Christ.

God's major change is called repentance, but no one can respond to the Lord acceptably without the present power and work of the Holy Spirit.

For God so loved the world that He gave His one and only Son so that anyone who surrenders and receives His sacrifice would experience God's standard of change. (John 3:16)

Beloved, do not allow yourself to become distracted by all of the arguments or the fine-sounding rhetoric of superior human wisdom. These will only move us away from the simplicity of trusting God and not our own perceptions.

As always, in His love, Pastor Ken Reed

SEVERED

To cut off; to separate; a sudden loss of contact or the abrupt isolation from; to disconnect.

On one hot and humid day in the Florida sunshine, a hissing noise and a rustling in a nearby brush caught the attention of a young boy as he played without a concern for his safety in the secure domain of his front yard.

However, without fully realizing it, there was imminent danger just about ten inches away. The noise along with a subtle and deliberate motion captured the young boy's attention. As he approached the brush curious to see the source of this noise, there, just in front of him, was a large black snake, which now moved into its defensive posture with tongue darting and eyes piercing, ready to strike. Suddenly and with no warning, the serpent's head was severed from its body. Seemingly out of nowhere, a garden hoe had come crashing down upon the creature. The young boy's mother, without his aware- ness, was ever vigilant in her watching and protecting her children.

No longer could the eyes and thought processes dictate to the snake's body any particular course of action. The separation was abrupt, sudden, and permanent.

Years later the young boy, now a fully grown husband and father, is walking through a beautiful park in North Carolina on a wide concrete walkway. It's a clear, warm, summer day.

Many people are walking, running, and biking along the path. As he is walking, he's talking on his phone with no concern for danger. As he is walking and talking, he accidentally stumbles on a branch along the path. As he turns to see the object that rolled under his foot, he's startled.

There, just a few feet behind him, is a poisonous snake. But amazingly, the snake's head was crushed. The snake was moving erratically in a confused motion. Its head has been flattened by his heel.

This time it was not his mother who rescued him from a ser- pent; *it was his heavenly Father.*

Every sensory connection in the snake was suddenly disrupted; all information that ruled and controlled all bodily input had now been permanently disconnected.

Consider these words from Scripture:

And the God of peace will soon crush Satan underneath your feet. (Romans 16:20)

Then the seventy returned, with great joy, saying, "Lord even the demons are subject to us, in your name." And Jesus said to them, "I saw Satan fall like lightning from heaven. Behold I give you the authority to trample underfoot serpents and scorpions and over all the power of the enemy, and nothing shall by any means hurt you. Nevertheless, do not rejoice in this that the spirits are subject to you, but rather rejoice because your names are written in heaven." (Luke 10:17–20)

Beloved, as new believers in Christ Jesus, we have a guarantee of protection. Many scriptures declare this to be the case (e.g., "'No weapon that sets itself against you and me shall be successful. This is our inheritance,' saith the Lord" (Isaiah 54:17)).

On many an occasion, our lives have been spared, some we are aware of and others we won't become aware of until we are standing in His presence. Beloved, be of a determined nature to trust His faithfulness toward His children.

As always, in His love, Pastor Ken Reed

POISON

A toxic substance causing illness or death; to advance internal injury to the body; the gradual eroding of health.

In John 10:10, Jesus distinguishes His purpose and function regarding our eternal fellowship with the Father: "The thief does not come except to steal, to kill, and to destroy, but I have come so that you may have life and an even more abundant life."

Everything and every aspect of Jesus is for our advantage. As what Romans 8:28 says, "God will allow every situation and circumstance to work together for our good," *even the disappointing and least desirable ones*.

But the evil one is opposed to God's purpose; there are no benefits for you and me coming from him. Every aspect of the thief relentlessly targets the accomplishment of God's perfect work and will in you.

So, he steals, kills, and destroys every good thing regarding your life.

Beloved, only living things can be killed, only things of value are stolen, and only the things that are effectively working for your good are targeted for destruction.

A reason for the seeming ease of Satan's effectiveness in God's people has <u>two parts</u>.

First *is his tailor-made / just-for-you scheme.* Second and equally effective *is the gradual nature of its implementation.*

<u>Like a page out of a mystery novel,</u> the femme fatale is a young and attractive nurse (Satan as an angel of light). The unsuspecting victim is her wealthy and aging husband (an unwise and careless believer). Over a period of approximately nine months, she administers minute amounts of arsenic.

The dosage is almost untraceable in the amounts and intervals given. The careless victim never considered the warning signs because of the gradual and diabolical process of the poison.

He attributed the increasing soreness of his joints and his vision's gradual loss to his age. His breathing became more complex, and his stomach and muscular aches increased to the point of his total incapacitation just before he died. This application of poison is highly effective.

Likewise, beloved, we face the enemy of our souls and are to be watchful and discerning of the signs and symptoms of poisoning.

Ephesians 6:11–12 says, *"Put on the full armor of God so that you may be able to stand your ground against all the wiles of the Devil. For we do not wrestle against flesh and blood, but against powers, the dark rulers of this age, and a host of spiritual wickedness in heavenly places."*

This is the only immunity against the subtle act of being poisoned by the enemy of our souls.

Ephesians 6 continues to instruct us *to put on the helmet of salvation and, "above all, taking the shield of faith by which, we can quench all the poisonous and fiery darts hurled at us by the enemy"* (Ephesians 6:16). The penetration by a dart and the poison's effects can be so gradual that it is not consistently recognized. *Many are presently infected unawares.*

Beloved, only as we allow God's Word to be the final authority in our lives can we discern the corruption from the poison working within us.

For God's word is full of life and all-powerful, it is sharper than any two-edged sword, and the only thing capable of separating the soul from the spirit, even unto the joints and the marrow. (Hebrews 4:12)

Oh Lord, have mercy on us and help us in these last hours.

As always, in His love, Pastor Ken Reed

DELIVERANCE

To transport from one specific location to another; to release someone or something to another; to set free from captivity, peril, or evil; to remove from danger or harm.

The book *Perfect Victim: The True Story of the Girl in the Box*, published in 1989, is the horrific and incredible story of Colleen Stan. It is a classic setting for an appreciation of deliverance. She was taken against her will at knifepoint, stripped, beaten, and held captive in a specially crafted box more than twenty hours a day for seven years.

She was removed approximately one to two hours a day for rape and/or torture. Over a period of time (approximately two to three years), she developed what's known as *Stockholm syndrome*.

Colleen was eventually assisted and rescued from her captor. She underwent intense therapy, name changes, and other reconstructive processes in an attempt to restore some sense of normalcy into her life.

January 1, 1863, began the third year of the Civil War. President Abraham Lincoln issued the *Emancipation Proclamation*, leading to the passing of the Thirteenth Amendment (deliverance).

The proclamation stated in short that "all persons held as slaves henceforth shall be freed."

Many slaves appeared to be eager to embrace the potentials of the proclamation. However, for most, there was little knowledge of the responsibilities or meaning of freedom. Some remained uncertain, skeptical, and fearful of departing from their familiar conditions.

They retained an underlying sense of commitment and loyalty to their captors. Many were apprehensive and, in some cases, suspicious of the promises of freedom.

Beloved, this is classic satanic manipulation. He is the master liar and thief.

For the evil one comes only to steal, kill, and destroy, but I have come so that you may have life, and a more abundant life.
(John 10:10)

God's motivation for sending His Son was and continues to be for the reacquiring of freedom in our lives, resulting in humanity being delivered from all the authority of the kingdom of darkness.

God always keeps and performs His promises to deliver us from evil. His one and only source is Jesus, His redemptive Lamb.

In 2 Corinthians 5:17, it says, "If any man be in Christ Jesus, he is without a doubt a brand-new Creation, the old has gone and the new has come."

Giving thanks to the Father, who has qualified or authorized us to become partakers of the inheritance with His saints, for He has Delivered us from the power and the authority of the kingdom of darkness and transferred us into the kingdom of His beloved Son.
(Colossians 1:12–13)

Now, for many believers, the reality of this finished work remains only a superficial point in their understanding. It is often engaged in apprehensively, with a disturbing number of sincere believers remaining uninformed about their responsibility *of mixing faith with God's precious promises.*

Beloved, even now God's freedom and deliverance is continuously available. But as with every other benefit, they must be received and made your own by faith.

Psalm 103:2–4 says, *"Bless the Lord oh my soul, and do not forget all of His benefits: who forgives all of your sins, who heal all of your diseases, who redeems [i.e., delivers] your whole life from destruction, crowning you with loving-kindness and tender mercies."*

As God's delivered people, do not allow familiar paths of satanic enslavement to become that which you continue to welcome in your life.

CONTRIVE

Deliberately created rather than arising as a natural occurrence; to be artificially orchestrated; forced, strained, or manufactured behavior.

If any man be in Christ Jesus, he is now created as a brand-new type of being. (2 Corinthians 5:17)

The original type of being we once were has ceased to exist because of Adam's sin. And not only so, but we also have become "the righteousness of God in Christ Jesus" (2 Corinthians 5:21).

This is clearly established in Scripture as God's <u>immutable</u> <u>truth</u>. So regardless of our feelings or experiences, good or bad, *we are God's property.*

Beloved, with that being the case, "the greater one lives in us" (1 John 4:4), and we are created, tailor-made, as it were, to have fellowship with and be led by the Holy Spirit.

For it is God who works in you both to will and to do of His good pleasure. (Philippians 2:13)

However, learning to come into agreement with the person and work of the Holy Spirit is a lifetime project.

Unfortunately for many believers, this process is not under- stood. So I make this next statement with great care and humility. Much of our kingdom work, <u>though genuinely sincere,</u> *is nothing more than a contrivance.*

Contrivance is *the use of skill to bring something about or to employ an artificial process or device in an <u>attempt to produce or reproduce that which is authentic or original</u>.*

There's a saying that goes something like this: T*he Holy Spirit is often imitated but never duplicated.*

For most, the intent is to be led by the Spirit, but in truth, we all tend to do what seems and feels right to us.

Many of us will work at the level of our educational development, our previous experiences, our learned concepts, or by employing motivational tactics.

Listen to the subtle distinction Paul makes in 1 Corinthians 2:1–5:

When I came to you, brothers, I did not come with a dependency on eloquent speech, in my presentation of the testimony about God. For I resolved [I was determined] to know nothing while I was with you except Jesus Christ and him crucified. I came to you in weakness and fear, and with much trembling [with no reliance on my giftedness, education, or previous experiences]. My message and my preaching were not with wise and persuasive words, but what the demonstration of the Holy Spirit's power, so that your faith might not rest on men's wisdom [human ability, talent], but in God's power.

Now I always like to make a clarification when it comes to this text. The word *power* here that Paul is referencing is not talking about miracles, healings, etc. The power he's referencing is the Holy Spirit's presence in the preaching of the gospel (i.e., he's simply saying, "I did not come with any kind of gimmick or contrivance. But I came weak and fearful in myself with an absolute dependency that the Holy Spirit would be your experience so that the faith that is developed in you is faith in God, not in any human ability").

Beloved, as we draw closer each day to the return of Jesus Christ, let's put an end to all contrivances. Practice daily being weak so that you might be strong in God's power.

And as in the book of Acts, let this comment be made of us: "And the people took note, that these men had been with Jesus" (Acts 4:13).

As always, in His love, Pastor Ken Reed

FEELINGS

Physical sensations, awareness, emotions, or sensitivity; an especially vague or irrational belief.

Feelings are marvelous and wonderful; they are the main source of vitality and passion in life. God has created and provided them in each of us.

They are readily cherished and treasured by us all, some more than others. Life as we presently know it would be all but dead if feelings were not an available experience for us.

Thank God for feelings! And *God, help us and deliver us from the dominance of our feelings!*

One of the most unreliable, inaccurate, and capricious sources for determining truth is human feelings.

Feelings do not know and cannot determine the truth.

Our feelings were not created to function as a filter or a screening source for truth.

Truth is only established and is valid within the context of a word from the Lord.

Let God be true and every man a liar. (Romans 3:4)

God is not a man that he should lie, nor the son of man that he should change his mind. Has he spoken, and then not acted, or has he ever made a promise that He has failed to bring the past? (Numbers 23:19)

Hebrews 6:18 says, "*It was by two immutable/unchangeable things in which it is impossible for God to lie.*"

Faith, if understood and limited to just these three verses, *has absolutely nothing to do with any feelings we may or may not experience.* "Pastor Ken, *my feelings are so strong. What's the cause, and what can I do about it?*" Beloved, as I've previously stated, *feelings are created and designed by God to foster a deep appreciation and thankfulness for Him in your life.*

Feelings are the centerpiece of the soul (consisting of *the mind* [i.e., our <u>intellect</u>], *the will* [i.e., our capacity to <u>make choices</u>], and lastly, *our emotions* [i.e., feelings]).

<u>This process functions akin to this</u>:

First, thoughts are formed in the mind, coming primarily from an outside source of information. This then produces an image. Once the image is clarified, *your emotions simply add the appropriate feelings to accommodate that image.*

The image in your mind is now infused with a sense of vitality and life. So now a decision or choice can be made. *This process occurs within a flash of a second and is repeated seamlessly within each of us all of our lives.* The Holy Spirit instructs us to continue to have our minds trans- formed with truth by faith, "setting our minds on things above, where Christ is seated at the right hand of the Father" (Colossians 3:1).

Beloved, it was never God's intention for our souls (i.e., our thoughts and feelings) to govern our lives. We are called and created to have *spiritual fellowship with God.*

We are spirit beings, we have souls, and we live in physical bodies. Do not allow the enemy to manipulate the order of God's kingdom in your life. Any disorder is a sign of the works of the flesh, *which is motivated by the prince of the power of the air.*

In light of our brief conversation, consider Hebrews 2:14:

"Inasmuch then as the children have partaken of flesh and blood, he himself likewise shared in the same, so that through death he might destroy him who had the power of death, that is, the devil."

As always, in His love, Pastor Ken Reed

STRUGGLE

To make forceful or violent efforts; to free oneself of restraint or constriction.

The concept that we as new creations in Christ Jesus are to be exposed to struggles and challenges has become disturbing and unsettling for many, *especially in large portions of the church in this nation.*

There is, just below the surface, an unspoken belief that as children of God, our lives are to be free of any encumbrances, interferences, or struggles of any kind.

Now few of us would actually acknowledge this position, but in reality, we all, on occasion, can become frustrated, impatient, and resentful when faced with opposition.

Many have become so offended and insulted that they have chosen to separate themselves from good churches, close relation- ships, employment, family members, and even marriages.

Beloved, few of us are willing and prepared to face the giants that are stationed on our path. Yet our loving, heavenly Father is the one who has marked out the path for us, we must believe that every giant and obstacle setting itself against us is, *technically, already defeated.*

Our struggle is not against flesh and blood, but against the rulers, powers, and authorities of darkness. (Ephesians 6:12 NIV84)

These rulers do not have authority over us in the same way that a dark room does not have authority over the smallest light when it is turned on. The smallest amount or weakest measure of light, on any occasion, can still pierce the darkness.

One of the Hebrew definitions of the word Satan is "the one who resists." His innate nature is to stand against you and me, but God has promised "that no weapon or demonic posture that stands against you shall prosper, but this is the inheritance of the servants of the Lord and their righteousness is of me" (Isaiah 54:17).

So be prepared, beloved, in your heart and attitude to stand your ground as a light who shines in dark places, joyfully demonstrating the kingdom of God.

A group of scientists in an experiment took two groups of fertilized chicken eggs (approximately fifty each) under controlled environments.

As the chicks began to hatch and the struggle of life ensued, one group was assisted by peeling back their shells. The other group was allowed to struggle without any assistance, *and a few perished.*

However, several weeks later, every chick of the assisted group died, not one survivor. But of the group that endured the struggle, most went on to develop normally (about forty-seven).

The assisted group missed the chance for the life-sustaining strength that is only acquired through struggle. *Beloved, let us not forget that this is warfare and that we are the invading army.*

The weapons that we fight with a not carnal, physical, or emotional, but they are mighty through God for the purpose of pulling down every strong- hold, and obstacle. (2 Corinthians 10:3)

And finally, my brethren, be strong in the Lord and in the power of his might, put on the full armor of God so that you can take your stand against all the schemes of the devil. (Ephesians 6:10–11)

As always, in His love, Pastor Ken Reed

CONCLUSION

The final part, especially in a period of time, activities, or events; the furthest and most extreme part or point (i.e., the end); to the full extent.

Beloved, there is a marked distinction between *a beginning and an ending*. As obvious as this may appear to be, it is not always easily discerned or willingly responded to, as you might imagine.

The capacity to distinguish, appreciate, and properly respond to a beginning and then to an ending is generally an indication that you are growing and maturing in God's process.

As we move closer to the conclusion of everything, especially in the context of the fulfillment of *prophetic and end-time events*, the focus of a maturing believer is being continuously refined and intensified.

There are preparations and positions taken toward the end of a project, which are simply unnecessary at the beginning or even during the process. But as one approaches a conclusion, there are fixed and detailed revisions that must be utilized.

The difference between a smooth conclusion of a wonderful flight or a fatal a crash landing is in adhering to those fixed details.

The beginning of the Super Bowl is filled with pageantry, hope, and expectation. There is, however, a sharp distinction in the strategy and objective between playing the game from the initial kick- off *and the final two-minute warning*, especially in a tight or tied score. It demands the introduction of specialty plays and skilled time management.

Every player is prepared and proficient in his specific area of expertise. There is a mindset and strategy that is only utilized during the conclusion of a game.

On these occasions, the difference between winning or losing is at stake. Focus is intensified, and with every action becoming more intentional, each individual gives great care to their assignment.

But I fear, that somehow, just as the serpent deceived Eve by his craftiness, so your minds may become corrupted from the simplicity that is in Christ. (2 Corinthians 11:3)

The tendency in our culture today is to slow down when approaching the conclusion. We've worked hard and long, we are exhausted, and finally the end of the shift is nearing, so some will begin to shut down, reducing their productivity and calling it a day.

The mindset of having increased focus and intensified effort unto the end has become awkward and highly unusual to some.

But as for you and me, let us take great care in our daily approach to life, for we are indeed lights shining into dark places.

For the end of all things is near, therefore, be serious and watchful in your prayers. (1 Peter 4:7)

And do this understanding the present time. For the hour has come for us to awake from our slumber, because our salvation is nearer now than when we first believed. The night is nearly over, the day is almost here, so let's put aside the deeds of darkness, and put on the armor of light.
(Romans 13:11–12)

Beloved, you and I are called and empowered by the Holy Spirit to be faithful until the end, and we are privileged to be the ones "on whom the end of the age has come" (1 Corinthians 10:11).

As always, in His love, Pastor Ken Reed

CONTRADICTION

Things that are a paradox or considered false; a position taken opposite the one already established.

Every satanic tactic, strategy, scheme, or technique utilized against you and me (the body of Christ) is tailor-made for each individual and is highly effective.

Its ability to affect either temporarily or in some instances permanently God's purpose in someone is startling. We have count-less examples of their effectiveness in people's lives, from Genesis to Revelation.

These tactics are so subtle that sometimes they can be easily overlooked, even by a more seasoned believer. All of these strategies are gift wrapped in just one kind of packaging. The packing is called "natural facts."

Just as "Jesus is the same yesterday today and forever" (Hebrews 13:8), likewise is the deceiver. From man's first encounter in the gar- den with the serpent to his final one, Satan's skillful use of natural facts to contradict God's kingdom order *is unaltered and relentless.*

Now, because we are created to have license in both dimensions, we have access and authority first in the *spiritual one* and second, *the physical.*

As new creations in Christ Jesus, our access into His spiritual kingdom is governed by faith, in the truth of God's Word.

Faith is a spiritual substance, and secondly, the evidence or proof that faith is present is unseen (i.e., no natural facts) (Hebrews 11:1 KJV).

However, as descendants of the first Adam with his residual "fallen nature," we are highly susceptible to the "captivating process" of embracing natural facts.

When caught off guard by this process, contradictions can easily employ extraordinary conflict, negatively impacting our fellowship with the Lord.

"Pastor Ken, *why are we vulnerable to this process*?"

First, I believe we've forgotten *our lives are not our own* (1 Corinthians 6:20). I'm continually recognizing in me the subtle presence of a desire for my own identity and pushing to become that person I see myself as.

Second (*I make these next comments tenderly and with great care*), I think in some instances we have become desensitized to God's supremacy. In addition to this spiritual fact, we have become dull, almost unconscious, in our perception of being submitted and respectful to Him.

And lastly and most importantly, we have forgotten that ultimately, God is sovereign.

His ways are above all, and His wisdom is unsurpassed.

Isaiah 40:25–3 says, "*To whom will you compare me? Or who is my equal? Do you not know? Have you not heard? The Lord God is the everlasting God, the creator of the ends of the earth. He will never grow tired or weary. Who can understand his wisdom? He gives strength to the weary and increases the power of the weak. Even youths grow tired and weary, and young men stumble and fall, but those whose hope is [continuously] in the Lord will renew their strength [constantly have their strength replenished]. They will soar on wings like eagles; they will run and not grow weary; they will walk and not be faint."*

Understand this, beloved: Even though He loves us, and we are his most beloved, *only God is God, and there is no other.* There is none like him.

As always, in His love, Pastor Ken Reed

UNLESS

Except or on the condition of (can be used as a conjunction or preposition).

In the English language, there are a variety of significant opportunities for the creative and sophisticated use of words.

Every word has within it the potential of imparting dramatic intensity and powerful emotion. Words can and do incite every range of human experience. This is not by chance or some untapped latent ability within humanity.

God Himself designed and established that everything from the beginning to the end as we know it began with a word: And God said, and it was so.

Our language (with all of its tenses, verbs, nouns, adjectives, etc.) can be exciting, motivating, and moving when someone is able to portray their feelings and desires proficiently through the use of words.

Beloved, consider the language used in these next few verses.

This truth is emphasized by the use of this conjunction: the simple word *unless*. What a power-filled conjunction.

Unless the Lord had given us help, how soon we would dwell in death. (Psalm 94:17 NIV84)

Unless your word becomes our delight, we will perish. (Psalm 119:92)

Unless the Lord had been on our side, we would have been swallowed up by our enemies. (Psalm 124:1–2)

The conjunction *unless* alerts us of our responsibility to intentionally connect our hope to this context, for *unless the Lord had intervened, we would have perished.*

Lastly, I'm convinced these two thoughts are clearly portrayed: first that our progress is not by human effort, talent, or any development of our intellect but only by His Holy Spirit; and second, "unless the Lord builds the house, they labor in vain who build it; Unless the Lord guards the city, the watchman stays awake in vain. *It is* [emphasis in the original] vain [a waste of time] for you to rise up early, to sit up late, to eat the bread of sorrows; for God gives his beloved sleep [i.e., rest in the midst of the storm]" (Psalm 127:1–2).

In closing, let us all choose to remember even in the face of a great giant (be it a pandemic, a financial crisis, or a violent attack like 9/11) the promise of God...

No weapon that has set itself against you [i.e., those belonging to Him] shall prosper [this promise of safety and protection even during the storm is an inheritance from him] ...and our righteousness is from him as well. (Isaiah 54:17)

It is not dependent upon our own actions or efforts; this is why the word *unless* is so crucial in this context, "for unless the Lord had intervened, we would have perished" (Psalm 19:92).

As always, in His love, Pastor Ken Reed

DEVELOP

To increase in size or stature; to advance in degree; and to clarify.

Being confident of this very thing, that he who has begun a good work in you will continue with it until the day of Jesus Christ. (Philippians 1:6)

For it is God who works in you both to will and to do of his good pleasure. (Philippians 2:13)

These two verses of Scripture should serve as a daily reminder to you and me so that we do not overtly focus our attention on ourselves or some other developed ability.

These two verses should also serve as a reminder that *it is God who began His perfect work in you and me and that it's God who faithfully continues that work (Philippians 1:6).*

His objective is for the completion of His plan, resulting in His fully developed and functioning kingdom within us.

When we focus on ourselves, we're acting as if the project and its management are now our responsibility. So, we are constantly struggling and attempting to finish the work God began.

This is simply not true, and actually, it's an indication of self-righteousness and a lack of genuine faith in "the finished work of Jesus Christ."

Considering a few basic steps of photography, this can help us gain a practical picture of God working in us.

First, a photo is taken. The film in your camera has now been exposed to light (Jesus Christ). Instantly an impression is burned on the film (your heart).

This image is always there; it never changes. This image can't be seen or perceived with our natural eyes (faith).

The film is removed from the camera and brought through a development process. The process includes the film being submerged into a variety of solutions (your life experiences).

As a result of the photographer (the Holy Spirit) placing the film in various solutions, a chemical reaction occurs (growth).

Now a blurry image (Godly character) begins to gradually appear on the film.

Then eventually, all within God's perfect time frame, the blurry image becomes clear to everyone.

We are being transformed into the image and likeness of Jesus Christ. (2 Corinthians 3:18)

We are also becoming lights that shine in darkness.

Beloved, God is greater than any problem we face, including "the poisonous arrows that flies through the day, and the terrors at night" (Psalm 91:5).

His promise is *you will see these things, but they will not come near you,* "for a thousand shall fall at your side and ten thousand at your right hand, but you are safe in the secret place" (Psalm 91:7)

I am God and there is no other, I am God and there is none like me. (Isaiah 46:9)

Beloved, give heed to the warning of Hebrews 4:2 *"that we should not be like those who did not benefit from the Gospel preached to them because they never mixed any faith with what they heard."*

In closing, beloved, *you must believe the things you think you know.*

You must believe that "no weapon that is formed against you will prosper" (Isaiah 54:17), that *He loves you, that He is with you, and that He's coming back for you.*

As always, in His love, Pastor Ken Reed

TIMING

The choice, judgment, or control of when something should be done; the regulation of speed to achieve effective performance.

In every professional sporting event, timing is critical. In baseball, for example, the difference between the average hitter and the clutch hitter is when he swings the bat. The primary distinction is not only contact but bat speed—in other words, timing. There is only a fraction of a second difference between a strike and a hit. It's all about timing.

In football, timing is even more essential; the quarterback has to employ patience and finesse for the completion of any pass with his receiver.

Can you glimpse the importance of patience, in waiting for the proper moment to take action? Again, in football, on most occasions the pass is thrown to a location where the receiver hasn't even arrived yet, so timing is critical.

Listen carefully to this word of the Lord in the context of our discussion:

> *Remember the former things, those of long ago; <u>I am God</u>, and there is no other, <u>I am God</u>, and there is none like me. I make known the end, from the beginning, from ancient times, what is*

still to come. <u>I say, my purpose will stand, and I will do all that I please</u>. From the East I summon a bird of prey; from a far-off land, a man to fulfill my purpose. <u>What I have said that I will bring about; what I have planned, that will I do</u>. (Isaiah 46:9–11)

God, who is the Alpha and the Omega and in whom there are no coincidences but a series of perfectly planned and timed events, has, from before the beginning, established a process where our lives are designed with the capability of responding to Him within the construct of His timing.

Ecclesiastes 3:1 declares, *"There is a time for everything and a season for every activity under heaven."*

Beloved, we must trust God's wisdom and timing, not our own judgments.

Verse 2 of Ecclesiastes 3 says, "A time to be born and a time to die." God has provided a preordained "span of life" so that each of one of us would have ample time to accomplish His plan and purpose for our lives.

Remember, beloved, we do not belong to ourselves. Our lives are not our own. We have been bought with a price for the purpose of satisfying God's design for each of us.

Verse 4 of Ecclesiastes 3 says, "A time to weep and a time to laugh; a time to mourn and a time to dance," and verse 6 says, "A time to search and a time to give up."

God's timing in regard to our lives is precise. Sometimes we can be a fraction of a second off and foul off God's pitch.

Are there a series of missed swings, fouled balls, etc. in your life?

Remember, <u>action and nonaction are equally valid</u>. It's never about me but always about Him, His ways, and His timing. We must be willing to accept that God's ways are not always as we imagine.

Where are you today, and what time is it in your life?

Beloved, please allow this to be a time of complete and purposeful surrender to our Lord so that our lives might declare: "Father, your kingdom come, and Your will be done" and "Not my will but Yours be done."

As always, in His love, Pastor Ken Reed

PRESSURE

A force exerted upon an object; the use of persuasion, influence, or intimidation to produce a desired behavior.

Generally speaking, any kind of pressure- or tension-filled set- tings are avoided by all of us. There are a few who boast of thriving in the presence of these conditions. However, they are unwittingly acknowledging that they are experiencing pressure as well.

We all tend to experience pressure when the requirement of a situation confronts our basic areas of comfort or when we are unwilling to venture beyond our personally established boundary. We then find ourselves being stressed and pressed.

We are fearfully and wonderfully made. (Psalm 139:14)

And so, because of the complexities and frailties of our humanity, the slightest thing from any situation can easily become a source of pressure (e.g., a crying baby, a job interview, a delivery that's a little late, going on a first or third date, a visiting with friends and relatives, a detour sign). Good, bad news, or just about any change in our daily routine can (and for many) become a source of pressure.

Because sources for pressure are unlimited, we spend much of our time and energy attempting to minimize if not avoiding completely any contact with pressure.

Jesus's invitation in Matthew 11:28–30 was this: "Come unto me all you who are weary and burdened [under enormous pressure], and I will give you rest. Take my yoke upon you and learn from me, for I am gentle and humble in heart, and you will find rest for your souls. My yoke is easy, and my burden is light." Did you notice that *His yoke and burden are light and easy, not heavy, wearisome, or burdensome?*

Beloved, only God knows the perfect balance and mixture of pressure and comfort to allow in our lives so as to encourage the development of His perfect will in you and me.

Because we are new creations in Christ Jesus, we are created to respond to "divine pressure." This is why "every situation works together for our good" (Romans 8:28).

When the Lord allows His pressure to work in us, we seldom identify or relate to it as being from God. So, on most occasions, we tend to complain and can become argumentative and even angry with Him.

In our rational evaluation, *we determined that everything is not working together for our good.* God is still, however, providing His grace for you and me to help bear His times of pressurized development.

As I understand it, *crystalline carbon* is one of the hardest minerals on the earth. In its natural form, it is an unappealing, unwanted, rock-shaped substance. But God, in His perfect wisdom, knows that by subjecting it to heat, time, and enormous pressure, this discarded and devalued substance undergoes a transformation, resulting in the production of the world's most beautiful and costly stones, *namely, diamonds.*

Every situation [all divine pressure], good or bad is working together for our good. (Romans 8:28)

Endure hardship [God's pressure], as discipline and as a good son. (Hebrews 12:7a)

No discipline [God's pressure] seems pleasant at the time, but painful. Later on, however it produces a harvest of righteousness and peace for those who were being trained by it.
(Hebrews 12:11)

Beloved, you and I must trust God in the fire, and under pressure, God's qualities and character are being developed in us so that we might become godly lights shining into dark places.

As always, in His love, Pastor Ken Reed

INOCULATE

The introduction of an active material into something, potentially altering its core; to introduce a microorganism into someone to prevent a disease.

The process of inoculation or vaccination is quite remarkable. Of all the various types of *medical research* pursued in almost every nation, none are as widely accepted or embraced as the endeavor to inoculate all against lethal diseases.

Inoculations are so mainstreamed in the consciousness of the cultures that most children, pets, dogs, cats, even cattle are all inoculated, and in many cases, these inoculations are nationally mandated. The now infamous COVID-19 virus, as of February 25, 2021, has reportedly had over five hundred thousand fatalities in this nation. The CDC and all of our top medical minds are fixated on neutralizing this disease by inoculation.

Now, hopefully, I won't sound like a radical fatalist, but there are many more lethal diseases of an even greater nature looming on the horizon.

Now learn this lesson from the fig tree: as soon as its twigs get tender and its leaves come out, you know that summer is near. Even so, when you see all these things, you know that it is near, right at the door. I'll tell you the truth, this generation will certainly not

pass away until, all these things have happened. Heaven and earth will pass away, but my words will never pass away.
(Matthew 24:32–35)

So, inoculations are more likely to be continued and accelerated. Inoculations are not without risk; there are, in fact, a countless number of adverse physical side effects being reported, including a disturbing number of fatalities. Inoculations are hopefully the results of arduous scientific research, being motivated by a concern for the relief of suffering and not just the company's bottom line.

Those who want to get rich fall into temptations, a trap, and into many foolish and harmful desires, which plunge people into ruin and destruction. For the love of money is a root of all kinds of evil. Some people, eager for money, have wandered from the faith, and pierced them- selves with many griefs. But you, man of God, flee from all this, and pursue righteousness, godliness, faith, love, endurance and gentleness. (1 Timothy 6:9–10)

The science of the process is something akin to the following: To prevent the infection of a life-threatening disease, a controlled amount of the bacteria itself is actually introduced into the blood-stream. The hope is that the "researched amount" for the safe infection is accurate in most participants. This small amount allows the body to fight off the bacteria, thereby creating a naturally occurring resistance to the bacteria.

Everything starts with blood. From the moment Adam sinned, his blood was infected with death and every side effect thereof, namely sickness, disease, etc. As I understand it, almost every disease can be evidenced in some form via blood test.

There are approximately five quarts of blood inside the average human body, and in approximately every twenty-three seconds, all five quarts are pumped throughout the circulatory system, allowing for every cell in the body to be refreshed through the presence of blood.

The life of all flesh is in the blood. (Leviticus 17:11)

As believers in Christ Jesus, we are to be well aware of Satan's subtle strategy of introducing a seemingly minute amount of sin into our lives, so small that we think we are immune to the lethal nature of it.

This is simply not true! Only as we <u>continually</u> trust the blood of Jesus are we are being <u>continuously</u> cleansed from every sin, known and unknown.

As always, in His love, Pastor Ken Reed

AIDS

Acquired immune deficiency syndrome.

We are indeed living in what many have characterized as being "the last days or the end of times."

I am certainly one who would wholeheartedly agree, especially considering these last thirty years. As of this present writing, we are in February 2021, and as I assess the years gone by, particularly the last twenty, the world has undergone such startling changes. At a stunning pace, many intelligent and well-versed people are finding it difficult to process and accept our present reality.

But mark this: there will be terrible times in the last days. People will be lovers of them- selves, lovers of money, boastful, proud, abusive, disobedient to their parents, ungrateful, unholy, and without natural affection, unforgiving, slanderous, without self-control.

[B]rutal, with no love for anything good, they will be treacherous, rash, conceited…singularly lovers of pleasure, rather than lovers of God…and finally having a form of godliness… but denying His power. Have nothing to do with them. (2 Timothy 3:1–5)

We could very easily spend the remainder of our time discussing how this one verse is a detailed depiction of today's mindset.

During the last thirty years, there has been an invasion of incredibly deadly, highly infectious diseases. It is not my intention to highlight any specific behavior as a cause for any of these. I am convinced that the side effects of Adam's sin include all sinful behaviors, diseases, sicknesses of all kinds, and eventually, death.

As I have briefly considered the strategic nature of these diseases and their means of avoiding the body's natural defenses, I was deeply struck by the demonic nature and function of many of the more famous (feared) diseases.

The flesh-eating Ebola virus is still impacting a large part of the world. Flu viruses like H1N1 and even the bird flu was recently transferred to a human host. All of the cancer family even heart, liver, and kidney disease are on the rise. *Are you starting to feel overwhelmed?*

Then there is the present star of the show, COVID-19. This one has literally crippled and altered the world. Every one of these diseases has the ability *to kill, steal, and destroy.*

One disease that seems to have a demonic nature at its core is the AIDS virus. This disease is intelligent and, in my opinion, is intentional and methodical in its process of infection.

God infused within our blood *white blood cells.* The white blood cells are the police and protectors of the human body. As I understand it, on average, there about twenty-five hundred to three thousand white blood cells present and at work in a healthy human body. The white blood cells are metabolizing, purifying, and eliminating all foreign bacteria and waste from the blood and, eventually, the body, promoting healthy bodily function and kingdom order.

The AIDS virus, when introduced into the bloodstream, specifically targets the white blood cells. The white blood cells naturally engage the virus, surrounding it in an attempt to neutralize and remove it from the blood. Once the white blood cells are within reach, the AIDS virus pierces the white blood cells, injecting its toxin, putting to death the cell and destroying its function. But even in the midst of the effective and prolific nature of these diseases, Jesus still offers life and the more abundant life.

As believers in Christ Jesus, you and I have received a spiritually healthy immune system. The satanic strategy to kill, steal, and destroy is continuously attempting to lure you and me into the place where death might pierce our hearts and inject itself into our lives.

"Set your heart on things above, where Christ is seated at the right hand of God" (Colossians 3:1), and *do not* focus upon or open your heart to the things of this world. They only produce death and disappointment.

As always, in His love, Pastor Ken Reed

ABOUT THE AUTHOR

Pastor Ken, as he is affectionately known, has pastored for about thirty years. He and his wife, Katie, have been married for forty-eight years. They have four sons, one daughter, and, at present, fourteen grandchildren.

Pastor Ken is well-known throughout the city of Worcester and the surrounding towns of Massachusetts as a gifted and anointed Bible teacher and communicator. His careful instruction in Scripture is respected from the island of Martha's Vineyard and throughout Cape Cod, where he started and for several years pastored the New Kingdom Worship Center. His consistent message of "Faith in the faithfulness, mercy, and grace of God" is impacting the lives of many.

www.ingramcontent.com/pod-product-compliance
Lightning Source LLC
Chambersburg PA
CBHW051205120626
46547CB00013B/1212